W9-ATF-135

Obama's Race to the White House

Dempsey J. Travis

No part of this publication may be reproduced or transmitted in any form or by any means, electronic or mechanical, including photocopy, recording, or any information storage and retrieval system, without permission in writing from the publisher.

Library of Congress Cataloging-in-Publication Data

Urban Research Press, Inc.

Copyright ©2008 Urban Research Press, Inc.
840 East 87th Street | Chicago, IL 60619 | USA
Printed in the United States of America
First Edition
ISBN: 0-941484-37-8

*This book is dedicated to
all of the black leaders and
politicians who believed in
change and made it happen.*

They paved the way.

-TABLE OF CONTENTS-

-INTRODUCTION-

"I'm asking you to believe. Not just in my ability to bring about real change in Washington... I'm asking you to believe in yours." – Barack Obama

When Senator Barack Obama announced he was entering the race for the Presidency, I thought of the young man dressed like an English fellow who had rented an office from me several years ago. I knew immediately that he would run a successful campaign and would show America the man we needed at this difficult time.

Many Americans are not aware of how deeply rooted African-Americans are in the history of United States politics. Men like John Jones started it all. He became a great orator and writer in the mid-1800s and used his skills to campaign for repeal of the Illinois Black Laws. Another early black politician was John Hanson, the nineteenth century Liberian Senator who championed the relocation of slaves to Liberia. They and other early black politicians like Edward H. Wright, Oscar DePriest, Mayor Edward J. Kelly, Alderman William L. Dawson, and Harold Washington led the way for those you will read about in this book.

Read the mystery regarding the six black presidents America has had in the past and why Barack Obama is not the nation's *first* black president. Discover the campaign details of each African-American who has run for President prior to Obama. Find out about the specifics of Obama's life and his work as a community organizer before his involvement in politics, his wife, and Hillary Clinton, his campaign rival before he won the nomination. Wrapping it all up is an in-depth chapter specific to Obama's life in politics and how he came to win the Democratic nomination with his "Yes We Can!" slogan and his speeches about hope and "Change We Can Believe In." Barack Obama has shown the American people that change is necessary and how he plans to bring it about, like so many leaders before him.

Come journey with me as we follow *Obama's Race to the White House*.

-ACKNOWLEDGEMENTS-

This book would not exist today without the members of my literary ensemble and their dedication and talents. Those members include: My wife, Mrs. Moselynne Travis, for being my motivation and support for the past sixty-two years; Kathy Maufas, my executive assistant, who comes to work each day with her ready-to-go attitude; Sherrol Glover, my knowledgeable senior researcher, who gathered hundreds of articles for this book and shed light on new possibilities; and a new member of the group, Heather Olson, for the cover illustration, editing, and typesetting.

-PREFACE: BARACK OBAMA—THE BEGINNING-

In January, 1993, I met Obama on the Southside of Chicago, Illinois. Obama had just been named by *Crain Magazine* as one of Chicago's Most Outstanding Business Leaders Under Age 40.

Shortly thereafter, a *Chicago Tribune* reporter called my office and said, "There are no young, black leaders standing in line in Chicago prepared to follow in the footsteps of the late Mayor Harold Washington and the subsequent interim Mayor Eugene Sawyer who was defeated by Richard J. Daley."

I assured the *Tribune* reporter that he was wrong, in that Jesse Jackson, Jr., and Barack Obama were standing in the wings ready to fly. Several weeks later, the same *Tribune* reporter wrote a laudatory story about Obama. The following week, Barack Obama stopped by the Dempsey J. Travis Realty office in Chatham at 840 East 87th Street, to thank me for bringing him to the attention of the *Tribune* people.

Obama is a tall, handsome young man in his late thirties. I recalled Obama being dressed like an English fellow. He carried an umbrella because it had rained that morning. He also wore a hat in Winston-Churchill style.

A week or two later, Obama returned to the Travis building and rented an office, Suite 201 in The Travis Realty Building in Chatham at 840 East 87th Street, located on the Southeast side of Chicago, Illinois, near Cottage Grove Avenue.

Mr. & Mrs. Travis with Barack Obama at a reception for Obama held by Atty. James Montgomery, January 2008.

In 2004, he was elected to the Illinois House of Representatives, and was subsequently elected to the Illinois United States Senate. In 2006, he took off like a rocket with a short fuse and in 2007, he announced his candidacy for the United States Presidency.

The same Suite, #201, in the Travis building had been previously occupied by the Former U. S. Senator Carol Moseley Braun, who decided to run for President of the United States in 2003.

The following are letters and memos from Obama, to myself:

Obama for Illinois
P.O. Box 802799
Chicago, IL 60680
Phone: (312) 427-6300
Fax: (312) 427-6401
www.obamaforillinois.com

facsimile transmittal

To: Mr. Dempsey Travis | Fax: 773-994-5191

From: Sen. Obama's Office | Date: 9/2

Re: Steering Committee | Pages:

CC:

☐ Urgent ☐ For Review ☐ Please Comment ☐ Please Reply ☐ Please Recycle

Notes:

September 2, 2003

Mr. Dempsey Travis
Travis Realty Company
840 E. 87th Street
Chicago, IL 60619

Dear Dempsey:

Thanks to the wonderful efforts of people all across the state, I am considered a top-tier candidate in the race to become Illinois' next United States Senator. We are meeting all of our financial and political goals, including having raised $1.4 million with nearly $1.1 million in cash on hand as of June 30th. This is in large part due to the counsel and advice that supporters like yourself have so generously provided.

Now, more than ever, I am asking for the direction and advice that only you can provide. With Labor Day and the petition drive fast approaching, the campaign is preparing to shift into high-gear. I am organizing a steering committee meeting of the area's top organizers, leaders and activists to assess recent campaign developments and form a strategy that will lead to the second half of the campaign being as successful as the first.

I have enclosed a poll memo to demonstrate how well positioned we are in the race as well as a list of everyone who has been invited to attend this meeting. Please review the memo as you prepare your ideas and suggestions.

The first meeting of the steering committee is taking place Monday, September 8th from 5:30 to 7:30 pm in the new Obama for Illinois headquarters at 310 S. Michigan Avenue, suite 1720. This meeting is extremely important, so please plan to join us. To RSVP, please call Randon Gardley at 312-427-6300. You may also e-mail your RSVP to rgardley@obamaforillinois.com.

I look forward to seeing you in attendance at this very important meeting.

Sincerely,

Barack Obama

P.O. Box 802799 • Chicago, Illinois 60680-2799
phone: 312/427-6300 • fax: 312/427-6401 • website: www.obamaforillinois.com

Paid for by Obama for Illinois. Federal law requires us to use our best efforts to collect and report the name, mailing address, occupation and name of employer of individuals whose contributions exceed $200 in a calendar year. Contributions are not tax deductible. Pursuant to the Bipartisan Campaign Reform Act of 2002, contributions are limited to $12,000 per individual for this election cycle. Corporate contributions are prohibited.

038

Barack Obama

March 2, 2007

Dempsey Travis
840 E 87th St
Chicago IL 60619

Dear Dempsey,

Recently, I was in New Hampshire and heard from a thirty-year-old young man who told me that the only politics he's ever known has been the divisive kind -- the politics that plays off our fears and blocks our progress and disappoints us year after year.

This is the kind of politics that's dominating Washington today, where partisans bicker, political points are scored and special interests try to turn our government into a game that only they can afford to play.

I'm running for President because I believe it's time to turn the page on these politics. I may not have been in Washington very long, but I've been there long enough to know that Washington must change. And I believe the American people are ready to make that change -- we're ready to solve the challenges of the 21st century and we're not willing to let the same small, divisive politics stand in our way anymore.

The good news is that there's another tradition of politics out there. A tradition that says we're all connected as one people -- that we have mutual responsibilities to each other. It's a tradition that says we have the power to close the gap between the world as it is and the world as it should be.

At every juncture in our history, this tradition has triumphed over cynicism. In the face of tyranny, a band of patriots brought an Empire to its knees. In the face of secession, we unified a nation and set the captives free. In the face of the Depression, we put people back to work and lifted millions out of poverty. We welcomed immigrants to our shores, we opened railroads to the west, we landed a man on the moon and we heard a King's call to let justice roll down like water, and righteousness like a mighty stream.

I have never believed the cynics who say we can't change this country -- that we have to accept America for what it is, instead of what it can be. I know we've overcome great obstacles before, and I have faith that with your help, we'll do it again. That's why this campaign can't only be about me. It must be about us -- it must be about what we can do together.

We'll need your honest advice, your energy and your time. And we need your financial support. Please send a gift of $1,000, $1,500, $2,300 to Obama for America and help us communicate our message of possibility. It's your energy that will keep us moving and your commitment that will change America. I know we can do it, and I can't wait to try.

Obama'08
BarackObama.com

Obama for America • PO Box 802798 • Chicago, IL 60680

Paid for by Obama for America

We've already taken the most important step. Your past support has already helped us rekindle a sense of energy and possibility in our politics. I can feel it out there, and I hope you can too. We've got people believing again. Now, we've got to make good on the hopes they've invested in us.

<u>We can change this country</u>.

I know there is another tradition of politics out there. It's a tradition I learned during my eight years in Springfield, Illinois, where I served in the state Senate. In a town found in the very heartland of America, where people of every race and background and belief came together, we learned to disagree without being disagreeable -- that it's possible to compromise so long as you know those principles that can never be compromised.

That's why we were able to reform a death penalty system that was broken. That's why we were able to give health insurance to children in need. That's why we made the tax system more fair and just for working families, and that's why we passed ethics reforms that the cynics said could never, ever be passed.

There's no reason we can't face today's challenges with this same kind of politics.

This begins with the biggest challenge we face today -- ending this war in Iraq.

If you're confused about the current debate over Iraq, you're not alone. People are wondering why political posturing in Washington continues as we get drawn deeper and deeper in Iraq. I hear it everywhere I go. People perceive that the most important issue of our day has become captive to sound bites and cable news chatter.

I was opposed to this war from the beginning because, in part, I believed it would lead to the devastating, open-ended occupation in which we find ourselves mired today. And that's why I've introduced legislation that would bring this tragic chapter in our history to a close. It's called the Iraq War De-Escalation Act. It makes the U.S. policy on Iraq crystal clear. It stops the escalation now and begins a redeployment to bring U.S. combat forces out of Iraq by March 31, 2008.

It's time to end this war so we can bring our troops home, refocus our efforts on the wider struggle against terrorism and start to tackle the challenges facing Americans here at home -- skyrocketing health care costs, a dependence on oil that threatens our future, schools where too many children aren't learning and families who are struggling paycheck to paycheck despite working as hard as they can.

What's stopped us from meeting these challenges is the failure of leadership, the smallness of our politics.

<u>The American people are hungry for a different kind of politics, and our campaign is about answering that call</u>.

I'm in this race, not just to hold an office, but to gather with you to transform a nation. I want to win that next battle -- for justice and opportunity. I want to win that next battle -- for better schools, better jobs and health care for all. I want us to build a better America.

So, I invite you -- I urge you -- to join your hopes with those millions of other Americans who still believe in what our country can be. I'm asking you to make this campaign the vehicle for your hopes and dreams. We need you to push us forward when we're right, and to let us know when we're not.

I need your help in this campaign. I also need your financial support. It's a reality of modern politics that it costs a great deal of money to communicate -- especially in a serious, substantive way. And so if you will, I ask that you take this moment to send a generous contribution of $1,000, $1,500, $2,300 or even more if you can possibly afford it, to **Obama for America**.

And if you will join me in this improbable quest, if you feel destiny calling, and see as I see, a future of endless possibility stretching before us; if you sense, as I sense, that the time is now to shake off our slumber, slough off our fear and make good on the debt we owe past and future generations, then I'm ready to take up the cause, march with you and work with you.

Together, let's begin.

Sincerely

Barack Obama

P.S. You and I also know hope alone can neither overcome our challenges nor embrace our potential. I embark on this campaign with high aspirations but no illusions. It's going to be tough. Change always is -- especially when we seek not simply new policies, but a new politics. I need your help to succeed. That's why I am asking you to rush a generous contribution of $1,000, $1,500, $2,300 to **Obama for America** today.

The life stories, when the presidential candidate tells them, have a common theme, the quest to belong.

A boy who wants to find his place in a family where he is visibly different: chubby where others are thin, dark where others are light.

A young, black man struggles for acceptance at an institution of privilege, where he finds himself growing so angry and disillusioned at the world around him that he turns to alcohol and drugs.

These have been the stories told about at least two character-shaping decades of U.S. Senator Barack Obama's life, a storyline that is largely shaped by his own best-selling memoir, political speeches and interviews.

But the reality of Obama's narrative is not that simple.

More than forty interviews with former classmates, teachers, friends and neighbors in his childhood homes of Hawaii and Indonesia, as well as a review of public records, show the arc of Obama's personal journey took him to places and situations far removed from the experience of most Americans.

At the same time, several of Obama's oft-recited stories may not have happened in the same way he has recounted them. Some seem to make Obama look better in the retelling, others appear to exaggerate his outward struggles over issues of race, or simply skim over some of the most painful, private moments of his life.

The handfuls of black students who attend Panahou School in Hawaii, for instance, say they struggled mightily with issues of race and racism there. Yet absent from those discussions, they say, was another student known as Barry Obama.

In his best-selling autobiography, *Dreams from My Father,* Obama describes having heated conversations about racism with another black student, "Ray." The real "Ray," Keith Kakugawa, is half black and half Japanese. In an interview with the *Chicago Tribune* on a Saturday, Kakugawa said he always considered himself mixed race, like so many of his friends in Hawaii, and was not an angry, young, black man.

He said he does recall long, soulful talks with the young Obama and that his friend confided his longing and loneliness. "But those talks," Kakugawa said, "were not about race, not even close." He added, "Obama was dealing with 'some inner-family turmoil' in those days, but it wasn't a race thing. Barry said his biggest struggles then were missing his parents, and his monumental feelings of abandonment. The idea that his biggest struggle was race is [bull]."

Then there's the copy of *Life Magazine* that Obama presents as his racial awakening at age nine. In it he wrote an article which included two photographs of an African-American man physically and mentally scarred by his efforts to lighten his skin. In fact, the magazines own historians said the *Life* article and the photographs don't exist.

Some of these discrepancies are typical of childhood memories: fuzzy in specifics, warped by age, shaped by writerly license. Others almost certainly illustrate how carefully the young man guarded the secret of his loneliness from even those who knew him best. And the accounts bear out much of Obama's self-portrait as someone deeply affected by his father's abandonment, yet able to thrive in a greatly disparate world.

Still, the story of his early years highlights how politics and autobiography are similar creatures; each is shaped to serve a purpose.

In its reissue, after he gave the keynote address at the Democratic National Convention in 2004, *Dreams From My Father* joined a long tradition of political memoirs that candidates have used to introduce themselves to the American people.

From his earliest moments on the national political stage, Obama has presented himself as having two unique qualifications: a fresh political face and an ability to bridge the gap between Americans of different races, faiths and circumstances. Among his supporters, his likeability and credibility have only been boosted by his stories of being an outsider trying to fight his way in. As much as he may have felt like an outsider at times, Obama rarely seemed to show it. Throughout his youth, as depicted in his first book, he always found ways to meld into even the most uninviting of communities. He learned to adapt to unfamiliar territory. And he frequently made peace, even allies with the very people who angered him the most.

Yet even Obama has acknowledged the limits of memoir. In a new introduction to the reissued edition of *Dreams From My Father*, he noted, "The dangers of writing an autobiography included; the temptation to color events in ways favorable to the writer… [and] selective lapses of memory."

He added, "I can't say that I've avoided all, or any, of their hazards successfully. It was a complicated time."

Hawaii had become a state only two years before Obama's birth, and there were plenty of native Hawaiians still deeply unhappy about it. The U.S. military was expanding on the Island of Oahu, home to the new capital of Honolulu. And a young, iconoclastic white woman, who had defied the social norm of the day by marrying a dashing black man from Kenya, was coping with the fact that her new husband essentially had abandoned her and their young child in 1963 to study at Harvard.

Oblivious to all of this was a perpetually smiling toddler the entire family called Barry. In snapshots, the boy is a portrait of childhood bliss. He posed at a life guard stand. He rode a bright blue tricycle with red, white, and blue streamers dangling from the handlebars.

In the weeks since Obama announced his intention to run for the White House, he routinely has suggested that his diverse background: raised for a time in the Third World, schooled at elite institutions, and active in urban politics, makes him the best-suited candidate to speak about rich and poor, black and white, mainstream voters and those utterly disenchanted with the political system.

Not as well known is the fact that the many people who raised him were nearly as diverse as the places where he grew up. There was his mother Ann, a brilliant, but impulsive white woman; his grandmother Madelyn, a deeply private, and stoically pragmatic Midwesterner; his grandfather Stanley, a loving soul inclined toward tall tales and unrealistic dreams.

"Looking back now, he would say he really is kind of the perfect combination of all of them," said his half sister, Maya Soetoro-Ng. "All of them were imperfect, but all of them loved him fiercely, and I believe he took the best qualities from each of them."

During her son's earliest years, Obama's mother, whose full name was Stanly Ann Dunham, because her father desperately had wished for a boy, attended college at the University of Hawaii. Known as Ann throughout her adult life, she kept to herself. She became estranged from her husband, Barack Obama, Sr., after his departure to Harvard and she rarely saw the group of friends that they had made at the University of Hawaii.

One of those friends, Neil Abercrombie, then a graduate student in the sociology department, frequently would see young Obama around town with his grandfather Stanley, who Obama called "Gramps."

"Stanley loved that little boy," said Abercrombie, now a Democratic congressman from Hawaii. "In the absence of his father, there was not a kinder, more understanding man than Stanley Dunham. He was loving and generous."

A close friend of Obama's from their teenage years, Greg Orme, spent so much time with Dunham that he, too, called him Gramps. Orme, recalled that years later, at Obama's wedding reception in Chicago, Obama brought the crowd to tears when he spoke of his recently deceased maternal grandfather, and how he made a little boy with an absent father feel as though he was never alone.

Madelyn Dunham, a rising executive at the Bank of Hawaii during Obama's Punahou days, was more reserved, but seemed to love having her grandson's friends over to play and hang out.

"Those were robust years full of energy, and cacophony and she loved all of it," Soetora-Ng said of her grandmother, who has lived alone since her husband died in 1992.

Ann and her son lived with the Dunhams in Honolulu until Obama was six. Then his young mother, now divorced, met and married an Indonesian student studying at the University of Hawaii.

In one family photo, before the mother and son moved to Indonesia, Obama walks barefoot on Waikiki Beach, arms outstretched, as though embracing the entire beautiful life around him, as the sailboat, the Manu Kai (bird of the sea, in English) was about to set sail behind him. Obama, too, was about to journey far from these familiar shores.

Obama has told the story which was one of the many watershed moments of his racial awareness time and again, in remarkable detail.

He is nine years old, living in Indonesia, where he and his mother moved with her new husband, Lolo Soetoro, a few years earlier. One day while visiting his mother, who was working at the U.S. Embassy in Jakarta, Obama passed time by looking through several issues of *Life Magazine*. He came across an article that he later would describe as feeling like an "ambush attack."

The article included photos of a black man who had destroyed his skin with powerful chemical lighteners that promised to make him white. Instead, the chemicals had peeled off much of his skin, leaving him sad and scarred, Obama recalled.

"I imagine other black children, then and now, undergoing similar moments of revelation," Obama wrote of the magazine photos in *Dreams From My Father*.

In fact, it is surprising, based on an interview with more than two dozen people who knew Obama during his nearly four years in Indonesia, that it would take a photograph in a magazine to make him conscious of the fact that some people might treat him differently because of the color of his skin.

Obama, who has talked and written so much about struggling to find a sense of belonging due to his mixed race, brushes over this time of his life in *Dreams From My Father*. He describes making friends easily, becoming fluent in Indonesian, in just six months, melding quite easily into the very foreign fabric of Jakarta.

The reality was less tidy. Obama and his mother joined her new husband, a kind man who later would become a detached heavy drinker and womanizer. Family members in Indonesia say their Jakarta neighborhood resembled a village, more than the bustling metropolis the city is today. Electricity had arrived only a couple of years earlier. Half the homes were old bamboo huts; the other half, including the Soetoro house, were nicer; with brick or concrete, and red-tiled roofs.

Former playmates remember Obama as "Barry Soetoro," or simply "Barry," a chubby little boy very different from the gangly Obama people know today. All say he was teased more than any other kid in the neighborhood primarily because he was bigger and had black features.

He was the only foreign child in the neighborhood. He also was one of the only neighborhood children whose parents enrolled him in a new Catholic school in an area populated almost entirely by Betawis, the old tribal landowning Jakarta natives who were very traditional Muslims. Some of the Betawi children threw rocks at the open Catholic classrooms, remembered Cecilia Sugini Hananto, who taught Obama in second grade.

Teachers, former playmates, and friends recall a boy who never fully grasped their language and who was very quiet as a result. Yet one word Obama learned quickly in his new home was *curang*, which means "cheater."

When kids teased him, Obama yelled back, "Curang, curang!"
When a friend gave him shrimp paste, instead of chocolate, he yelled, "Curang, curang!"

Zulfan Adi was one of the neighborhood kids who teased Obama most mercilessly. He remembers one day when young Obama, a hopelessly upbeat boy who seemed oblivious to the fact that the older kids didn't want him tagging along, followed a group of Adi's friends to a nearby swamp.

"They held his hands and feet and said, 'One, two, three' and threw him in the swamp," recalled Adi, who still lives in the same house where he grew up. "Luckily he could swim. They only did it to Barry."

The other kid would scrap with him sometimes, but because Obama was bigger and better-fed than many of them, he was hard to defeat.

"He was built like a bull. So we'd get three kids together to fight him," recalled Yunaldi Askier, a former neighborhood friend. "But it was only playing."

Obama has claimed on numerous occasions to have become fluent in Indonesian in six months. Yet those who knew him disputed that.

Israella Pareira Darmawan, Obama's first grade teacher, said she attempted to help him learn the Indonesian language by going over pronunciation and vowel sounds. He struggled greatly with the foreign language, she said, and with his studies as a result.

The teacher, who still lives in Obama's old neighborhood, remembers that he always sat in the back corner of her classroom. "His friends called him 'Negro,'" Darmawan said. The term wasn't considered a slur at the time in Indonesia.

Still, all of his teachers at the Catholic school recognized leadership qualities in him. "He would be very helpful with friends. He'd pick them up if they fell down," Darmawan recalled. "He would protect the smaller ones."

Third-grade teacher Fermina Katerina Sinaga has perhaps the most telling story. In an essay about what he wanted to be when he grew up, Obama wrote, 'he wanted to be president,'

Sinaga recalled. "He didn't say what country he wanted to be president of, but he wanted to make everybody happy."

When Obama was in fourth grade, the Soetoro family moved. Their new neighborhood was only three miles to the west, but a world away. Elite Dutch colonists once lived there; the Japanese moved in during their occupation of Indonesia in World War II. In the early 1970s, diplomats and Indonesian businessman lived there in fancy gated houses with wide paved roads and sculpted bushes.

Obama never became terribly close with the children of the new school - this time a predominantly Muslim one - where he was enrolled. As he had at the old school, Obama sat in a back corner. He sketched decidedly American cartoon characters during class.

"He liked drawing Spider-Man and Batman," said another friend, Widiyanto Hendro Cahyono. "Barry liked to draw heroes."

Then one day about a year after he had arrived, Obama was gone.

"Suddenly we asked, 'Where's Barry?'" remembered Ati Kisjanto. "And we were told he had already moved away."

CHAPTER 1 – THE BLACK PRESIDENTS SET PRECEDENCE

The nation's first six black presidents.

Senator Barack Obama, presidential Democratic nominee, campaigned to become the nation's first black president – that is, he campaigned to become the nation's first *openly* black president. If speculation and evidence is correct, America may have already nominated a black president in the past on more than one occasion. In fact, this has happened on six occasions since the United States became a country.

Thomas Jefferson was the nation's third elected president, serving in the title from 1801 to 1809. He was born in 1743, in Albemarle County, Virginia to a father who was a planter and a surveyor and to a mother who had high social standing. He studied at the College of William and Mary and continued on to read law. He was described by Dr. Leroy Vanghn to be the "son of a half-breed Indian squaw and a Virginia mulatto father." He was sandy-haired and freckled and awkwardly tall but he was the first black president. Jefferson was said to have destroyed all documentation leading to his mother. "The Johnny Cake Papers" of 1867 stated that when his mother died, he destroyed all of her papers, portraits, and personal effects. He also requested that every person return the letters they had received from his mother. Considering the more than 18,000 documents Jefferson saved regarding himself, in destroying documentation attached to his mother, he must have been trying to hide something. In recent years, it was revealed by the family of Thomas Jefferson that he was the father of several children born to Sally Hemmings, a slave on his plantation.

The nation's seventh president was President Andrew Jackson. He was in office between 1829 and 1837. He was born in the Carolinas on a backwoods settlement in 1767. Historian J.A. Rogers wrote in his book, *Five Black Presidents*, that Andrew Jackson, Sr. had died before Andrew Jackson, Jr. was born. After Jackson, Sr.'s death, the president's mother went to live on the Crawford farm and conceived Andrew Jackson, Jr. with one of the black slaves who lived on the farm. An article in *The Virginia Magazine of History* stated that Jackson was the son of an Irish woman who had married a black man. It went on to state that Jackson's oldest brother had been sold as a slave. Jackson went on in life to become very prosperous and to own slaves himself.

Abraham Lincoln was born on February 12, 1809, in Hardin County, Kentucky, and was the sixteenth president. He served as president between 1861 and 1865. While both of his given parents were born in Virginia, his mother was alleged to have come from an Ethiopian tribe. Vanghn wrote that Lincoln had very dark skin and coarse hair. His appearance and heritage sparked controversy during his campaign as he was nicknamed "Abraham Africanus the First" by his opponents. Political cartoons depicted him as being black. In fact, it could be that his father was not really his father at all. Lincoln's law office partner, William Herndon, said that Lincoln's father, Thomas Lincoln, could not have been Lincoln's father. He became sterile after suffering through childhood mumps and was later castrated. As president, Abraham Lincoln issued the Emancipation Proclamation on January 1, 1863, which declared forever free the slaves within the Confederacy. He was assassinated by John Wilkes Booth at Ford's Theater in Washington on April 14, 1865, which was Good Friday.

The president in office between 1921 and 1923 was Warren Harding, the twenty-ninth president. He was born near Marion, Ohio in 1865 and died of a heart attack in August of 1923. Albert B. Southwick, a columnist for the Worcester Telegram & Gazette in Massachusetts, said President Harding never denied his ancestry, which came from black relatives between both of his parents, including his great-grandmother, Elizabeth Madison Harding. When Harding was asked by a friend about his ancestors, he reportedly said, "How do I know? One of my ancestors may have jumped the fence." William Chancellor, a professor of economics and politics at Wooster College in Ohio, alleged that the Justice Department agents bought and destroyed all copies of his book in which he speaks about Harding's black heritage. Harding suffered from a nervous breakdown at the age of twenty-four and spent some time in a sanitarium. In the years between 1889 and 1901, he went to the J.P. Kellogg sanitarium in Battle Creek, Michigan five times to recover from fatigue, nervous illnesses, and overstrain. Many speculate that his illness was due to the pressures of not fully disclosing his black heritage and being forced to live as "white." Mrs. Marsha Stewart, a sixty-year-old teacher in suburban Detroit, Michigan, said she does not need any professional research to remind her that President Harding is her cousin. She claimed it is something the family has always been aware of but that they never spoke publicly about.

Calvin Coolidge was in office as the nation's thirtieth president, serving between 1923 and 1929. He was born on the fourth of July, 1872, and was the son of a village storekeeper. He is said to have been proud of his heritage and claimed his mother's dark complexion was because of her mixed Indian ancestry. Auset Bakhufu, author of *The Six Black Presidents,* disputed this claim and said in her book that by the 1800s, the Indians of the New England region were rarely pure Indian because they had so often mixed with blacks. Coolidge's mother's maiden name was "Moor," which is the name given to blacks in Europe just as "Negro" was used in America. It has been concluded that Coolidge was part black.

President Dwight David Eisenhower was born in Texas in 1890, and was raised in Abilene, Kansas. He was the third of seven sons and served as the nation's president from 1953 to 1961. Eisenhower's mother, Ida Elizabeth Stover, was a mulatto woman. As president, Eisenhower made military integration laws a reality after they had not previously been put into place. As the desegregation of schools began, he ordered the complete desegregation of the Armed Forces, writing, "There must be no second class citizens in this country." Eisenhower was the last "black" president elected.

The wedding of Eisenhower's parents

Before these great leaders in history became presidents, a man named John Hanson was elected by the Constitutional Congress to be the first President of the United States in Congress Assembled, from November 5, 1781 to November 3, 1782. The Presidents of the United States in Congress Assembled are not commonly known because the Articles of Confederation did not work well. The individual states had too much power and nothing could be agreed upon. Maryland refused to sign this document until Virginia and New York ceded their western lands. Maryland was afraid that these states would gain too much power in the new government from such large amounts of land. Once the signing of the Articles took place in 1781, a leader was needed to run the country. John Hanson was chosen unanimously by Congress (which included George Washington). In fact, all the other potential candidates refused to run against him, as he was a major player in the revolution and an extremely influential member of Congress. As the first leader, Hanson had quite the shoes to fill. No one had ever been in such a role of leadership before. He took office just as the Revolutionary War ended. Almost immediately, the troops demanded to be paid. As would be expected after any long war, there were no funds to meet the salaries. As a result, the soldiers threatened to overthrow the new government and put Washington on the throne as a monarch. All the members of Congress ran for their lives, leaving Hanson as the only guy left running the government. He somehow managed to calm the troops down and hold the country together. If he had failed, the government would have fallen almost immediately and everyone would have been bowing to King Washington. In fact, Hanson sent 800 pounds of sterling silver by his brother Samuel Hanson to George Washington to provide the troops with shoes. Hanson ordered all foreign troops off American soil, as well as the removal of all foreign flags. This was quite the feat, considering the fact that so many European countries had a stake in the United States since the days following Columbus. The Articles of Confederation only allowed a President to serve a one year term during any three year period. Six other leaders were elected after him - Elias Boudinot (1783), Thomas Mifflin (1784), Richard Henry Lee (1785), Nathan Gorman (1786), Arthur St. Clair (1787), and Cyrus Griffin (1788) - all prior to Washington taking office.

There is much speculation around the World Wide Web that John Hanson may have been a black man because of his Moorish background. The term *Moor* is sometimes used to describe any denizen of North Africa. In fact, it is rumored that John Hanson is on the back for the two-dollar bill. The picture on the two-dollar bill is a painting of the Committee of Five presenting the Declaration of Independence to the President of the Continental Congress of the United Colonies. In the image is a man who has dark skin and who is wearing a powdered wig while sitting at the table just to the left of the men standing in the center of the engraving. However, John Hanson was never a member of the Continental Congress. He did not serve as a Delegate until 1781, after the Continental Congress was replaced by the United States in Congress Assembled by the Constitution of 1777. The 1776 Delegate circled in the photo below is

A dark-skinned man on the back of the two-dollar bill – who is it?

believed by some to be John Hanson, the black Moor. It is worth noting that in the original painting hanging in the United States Capitol Rotunda, the dark-skinned man does not appear.

Because there was no photography in 1783, when John Hanson died, there are no photos of the leader. There is a painting of a white man named John Hanson and there is a sixth-plate daguerreotype of a black man named John Hanson. It is speculated that the painting is John Hanson, President of the United States in Congress Assembled. The sixth-plate daguerreotype is circa 1856, and is said to be John Hanson, the nineteenth century Liberian Senator from Grand Bassa County, who championed the relocation of slaves to Liberia. Whether the leader John Hanson, President of the United States in Congress Assembled, was black or white remains under investigation by many historians.

It is not surprising or unbelievable that the United States has seen six black presidents up to date. As millions of Americans are now taking DNA tests, they are discovering an astounding truth: according to some tests, one-third of white Americans will possess between two and twenty percent African genes. The majority of black Americans possess some European ancestors. The large difference between Barack Obama and most of the former "black" presidents is that their family histories were not fully acknowledged by themselves or by others. Although Obama is African-American, coming from a white mother and a black father, he strongly resembles his Kenyan father *and* his white grandfather. Obama is not only open about and proud of his ancestry, but most people also recognize and acknowledge him as a black man. This reason alone is why the majority of people will identify Obama as the first black president of the United States.

Controversy surrounds John Hanson: Was he the white man in the painting left or the black man in the daguerreotype right?

CHAPTER 2 – BARACK OBAMA—LIFE BEFORE POLITICS

Stanley Ann Dunham Soetoro with son Barack in Hawaii

There was a time before Obama wore tailored suits - when his wardrobe consisted of $5 military-surplus khakis and used leather jackets, and he walked the streets of Manhattan for lack of bus fare. It was a time well before the political arena beckoned, when his friends thought he might become a writer or a lawyer, but certainly not the first African-American man with a real chance to become president of the United States.

Barack Hussein Obama, Jr. was born August 4, 1961, in Honolulu Hawaii. His father was Barack Obama, Sr. and was Kenyan and his mother was Stanly Ann Dunham and was born in Wichita, Kansas. His parents met while attending the University of Hawaii, where his father had won a scholarship that allowed him to leave Kenya to pursue his dreams in Hawaii. At the time of his birth, Obama's parents were students at the East–West Center of the University of Hawaii at Manoa.

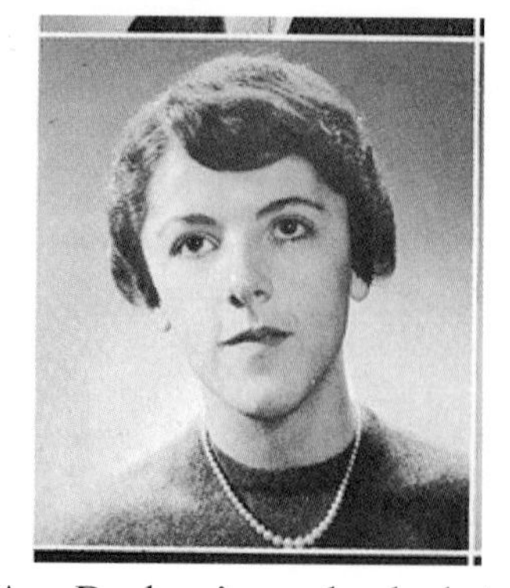

Ann Dunham's yearbook photo.

Barack Obama's parents

In 1963, when Barack, Jr. was just two-years-old, his parents separated and later divorced. His father returned to Kenya after receiving his Ph.D. from Harvard. Four years after that, in 1967, his mother married an Indonesian man named Lolo Soetoro. The family then moved to Jakarta and Ann gave birth to Obama's half-sister, Maya Soetoro-Ng. Obama attended schools in Jakarta where the classes were taught in the Indonesian language.

It was 1971 when Obama moved back to Hawaii to live with his grandparents, Madelyn and Stanley Dunham, and attend Panahou School. He was commonly known as "Barry" during his early years. He was in the fifth grade at Panahou Academy and was only one of three black students in the school. This experience caused Obama's first awareness of racism and what it meant to be an African-American. He struggled to reconcile with the social perceptions of his multiracial heritage. Also in 1971, he saw his biological father for the first time since he had left and also for the last before his father died in a car accident in 1982.

Obama's features are similar to those of a younger Stanley Dunahm.

Barack Obama, Jr. with his father in 1971 – the only time he saw his father after age two.

Punahoe School, via Associated Press

Mr. Obama, top right, in his high school senior yearbook

His mother returned from Indonesia to Hawaii in 1972 for several years before returning back to Indonesia for field work. Barry Obama graduated from high school in 1979. As an adult, Obama admitted that during high school, he used alcohol, cocaine, and marijuana. He described his drug use as his greatest moral failure at the Saddleback Church Civil Forum on the Presidency.

After high school, Obama studied at Occidental College in Los Angeles for two years. He was only eighteen when he arrived at the small liberal arts college nicknamed "Oxy." His freshman roommates were Imad Husain, a Pakistani, who's now a Boston banker, and Paul Carpenter, now a Los Angeles lawyer. Carpenter recalled Obama as "a good bodysurfer" who had "a funky red car, a Fiat," and who also played intramurals - flag football, tennis and water polo. "He was an athletic guy. He was gifted in that regard," said Carpenter. He also remembered Obama being "super bright. He could get through the course work in a fraction of the time it took me." Obama had an international circle of friends - "a real eclectic sort of group," says Vinai Thummalapally, who himself came from Hyderabad, India. As a freshman, he quickly became friends with Mohammed Hasan Chandoo and Wahid Hamid, two wealthy Pakistanis. There were others, Thummalapally recalled: a French student and both black and white Americans, including Jon K. Mitchell, who later played bass for country-swing band Asleep at the Wheel. Mitchell remembers that Obama wore puka shell necklaces all the time, though they were not in style, and that "we let it slide because he spent a lot of time growing up in Hawaii." The friends got together often to watch basketball games - they were Lakers fans - and eat the southern Indian food that Thummalapally cooked with his cousin. There was serious talk, too. Obama had concerns about U.S. foreign policy - including the failed hostage rescue mission in Iran under Jimmy Carter, and American support of the Contras in Latin America. Thummalapally lived with Obama the summer of 1980. The two ran together daily, three miles in the early morning, often chatting about their dreams. Thummalapally wanted to start a business back home; Obama talked about helping people. "I want to get into public service," he recalls Obama saying. "I want to write and help people who are disadvantaged." Obama's friends remember a good student with a sharp mind and unshakable integrity, a young man who already had a passion for the underprivileged. The young man remembered by Margot Mifflin, a friend from Occidental who is now a professor of journalism at Lehman College in New York, was "an unpretentious, down to earth, solidly middle-class guy who seemed somewhat more sophisticated than the average college student. He was slightly reserved and deliberate in a way that I sometimes thought betrayed an uncertainty."

In 1981, he transferred to Columbia University in New York City and graduated in 1983, with a degree in political science and a specialization in international studies. Obama's friend, Sohale Siddiqi, shared a story about Barack about the two of them walking Siddiqi's dog, a pug named Charlie, on Broadway. In his words, a large, scary bum approached them and stomped on the ground near the dog's head. Siddiqi was angry and wanted to confront the bum. When he did so, the bum turned threatening. But Ivy League educated Barack Obama intervened. Siddiqi recalled how Obama "stepped right in between…He planted his face firmly in the face of the guy. 'Hey, hey, hey,' and the guy backpedaled and we kept walking."

Obama's memoir, *Dreams From My Father,* talks about this time in his college years, but not in great detail; Siddiqi, for example, is identified only as "Sadik" - "a short, well-built Pakistani" who smoked marijuana, snorted cocaine and liked to party. While Obama has acknowledged using marijuana and cocaine during high school in Hawaii, he writes in the memoir that he stopped using soon after his arrival in New York. Siddiqi says that during their time together in New York, Obama always refused his offers of drugs. In his memoir, Obama recalls fasting on Sunday; Siddiqi says Obama was a follower of comedian-activist Dick Gregory's vegetarian diet. "I think self-deprivation was his schtick, denying himself pleasure, good food and all of that." Siddiqi has not kept in touch with Obama.

Obama during his Columbia years.

His has been a difficult road; years after his time with Obama, Siddiqi says, he became addicted to cocaine and lost his business. But when he needed help during his recovery, Obama - the roommate he drove away with his partying, the man he always suspected of looking down at him - gave him a job reference. So yes, he's an Obama man, too. Witness the message on his answering machine: "My name is Hal Siddiqi, and I approve of this message. Vote for peace, vote for hope, vote for change, and vote for Obama."

After graduation, Obama worked for Business International Corporation and New York Public Interest Research Group. He then, in 1985, signed on as a full-time community organizer with a church-based group, Developing Communities Project, and moved to Chicago. This three-year stretch as a grassroots organizer figured prominently in his own narrative of his life. It was here that he realized it would take changes in our laws and politics to truly improve the lives of the people in these impoverished neighborhoods. He worked as a community organizer with low-income residents in Chicago's Roseland community and the Altgeld Gardens public housing development on the city's South Side. During his three years as the DCP's director, its staff grew from one to thirteen and its annual budget grew from $70,000 to $400,000, with accomplishments including helping set up a job training program, a college preparatory tutoring program, and a tenants' rights organization in Altgeld Gardens. Obama also worked as a consultant and instructor for the Gamaliel Foundation, a community organizing institute.

While working as a grassroots organizer, Obama joined the Trinity United Church of Christ and met Reverend Jeremiah Wright who, in 1988, gave a speech titled "Audacity to Hope." Obama later used this as the title of his second book.

Obama entered Harvard Law School in late 1988, and was selected as an editor of the *Harvard Law Review* based on a writing competition and his grades. During his second year, he was elected president of the *Law Review*. It was a full-time volunteer position as editor-in-chief and supervisor to the *Law Review's* staff of eighty editors. He was the first black president for *Law Review* in its entire 104-year history. He then graduated *magna cum laude* from Harvard in 1991 and returned to Chicago. He began directing Project Vote, a grassroots campaign that registered nearly 150,000 black voters for the 1992 elections.

Obama met his wife, Michelle, in 1988, when he was a summer associate at the law firm Sidley & Austin in Chicago. They were married on October 18, 1992. He then went to work as an associate for Miner, Barnhill & Galland, a law firm in Chicago. He took on employment discrimination claims and voting rights cases. He also, at this time, joined the University of Chicago Law School, teaching constitutional law part-time.

In 1995, Barack Obama published his first book, a memoir of his youth and early career entitled *Dreams From My Father*. The publicity from his election as the first black president of the *Harvard Law Review* led to a contract and an advance to write a book about race relations. He had planned to finish the book in one year's time but it took much longer as the book evolved into his personal memoir. Obama and Michelle travelled to Bali, where he was able to work for several months without interruptions. The book was re-printed in 2004 with a new preface and an annex containing the text of his 2004 Democratic Convention keynote speech.

The audio book edition earned Barack the 2006 Grammy Award for Best Spoken Word Album. The following is an excerpt:

> I know, I have seen, the desperation and disorder of the powerless: how it twists the lives of children on the streets of Jakarta or Nairobi in much the same way as it does the lives of children on Chicago's South Side, how narrow the path is for them between humiliation and untrammeled fury, how easily they slip into violence and despair. I know that the response of the powerful to this disorder -- alternating as it does between a dull complacency and, when the disorder spills out of its proscribed confines, a steady, unthinking application of force, of longer prison sentences and more sophisticated military hardware -- is inadequate to the task. I know that the hardening of lines, the embrace of fundamentalism and tribe, dooms us all.
>
> And so what was a more interior, intimate effort on my part, to understand this struggle and to find my place in it, has converged with a broader public debate, a debate in which I am professionally engaged, one that will shape our lives and the lives of our children for many years to come.

Barack's Extended Family

In mid-1988, he traveled for the first time to Europe for three weeks then Kenya for five weeks where he met many of his Kenyan relatives for the first time. His father, Barack Obama, Sr., was born of Luo ethnicity in Nyanza Province, Kenya and grew up in the rural village of Nyangoma Kogalo, which is in Western Kenya near the shores of Lake Victoria. He herded goats before winning a scholarship to study in the US. He is now buried in that same quiet village.

Obama's grandmother, uncle and a handful of cousins still live in and around Nyangoma Kogalo, living the same simple life they have for generations. They do not have a television, but still managed to closely monitor election progress and pray for his victory. His grandmother, affectionately referred to as "Mama Sarah," told a CNN reporter, "He's a good listener and if he's given a chance, he will work hard for America." When asked what she thought of Hillary Clinton, Mama Sarah replied with a diplomacy her grandson would be proud of, that the election is a contest and the best man or woman should win.

Another enthusiastic supporter of Barack Obama's presidential campaign was his half-sister Maya Soetoro-Ng. After Obama's mother divorced Barack Obama Sr., she married Lolo Soetoro and had Maya in Indonesia. They moved back to Honolulu where Obama had been born. Although they are nine years apart, the siblings remain close. Maya credits Obama with helping her make good decisions and focusing on her strengths after her father died in 1987 -

but she also credits their mother, Ann Dunham, with instilling in Obama a love of public service and community organization. "She was an immense woman," Maya said of their mother. "She embraced everybody. There was so much good in her that there wasn't any room for smallness or meanness or violence." Today, Maya is a teacher and professor in Honolulu. She and her husband, Konrad Ng, have a 2-year-old daughter, Suhaila.

George Obama is, according to his birth certificate, Barack Obama's half-brother. He lives in a small house in Huruma with his mother's extended family. In Barack's memoir, *Dreams From My Father,* he describes meeting George as a "painful affair." The book is popular in Nairobi and can be found in most supermarkets there. Obama looks back at his struggles to reconcile with a Kenyan father who left him and his mother when he was a toddler. Like Barack, George hardly knew their father – Barack Obama, Sr. died in a car accident when George was six months old.

"I think I wanted to learn about my father the same way he did," George Obama said. "He came here searching for his roots, and I was also trying to find my roots."

Barack Obama's brother, George.

Senator Barack Obama greeting crowds in Nairobi in August, 2006.

CHAPTER 3 – MICHELLE OBAMA

Michelle LaVaughn Robinson Obama is married to Barack Obama, formerly a junior United States Senator from Illinois who won the 2008 election for United States President.

Michelle LaVaughn Robinson was born on January 17, 1964, to Frasier Robinson, a city pump operator and Democratic precinct captain, and Marian Robinson, a secretary at Spiegel's catalog store. Michelle was raised in a one-bedroom apartment on the top floor of a classic Chicago brick bungalow, now surrounded by a chain link fence, in the South Shore neighborhood of Chicago, Illinois. Her mother still lives there, behind burglar-proof wrought iron doors and secured windows, poised above a hedge of clipped yews.

She has a brother, Craig, who is sixteen months older than she is. Both children skipped the second grade. She graduated in 1981, from Whitney M. Young Magnet High School in Chicago's West Loop. She majored in Sociology with a minor in African American studies at Princeton University, graduating *cum laude* in 1985, and obtained her Juris Doctor degree from Harvard Law School in 1988.

For three years after law school, Michelle worked as an Associate in the area of marketing and intellectual property at the law firm Sidley & Austin in Chicago. In 1989, while working at the firm, she was assigned the role of advisor to a summer associate from Harvard, Barack Obama.

Barack reportedly didn't have much interest in corporate law, but he did have a lot of interest in Michelle. After refusing to go out with him for a month, she agreed to go to dinner and then to a movie, *Do the Right Thing,* on their first date. She said "she fell in love with him for the same reason many other people respect him, his connection with people."

After spending a few years in the private sector, Michelle left the corporate law world in 1991, to pursue a career in public sector, working first in the Chicago city government as an Assistant to the Mayor and then as Assistant Commissioner of Planning and Development of the City of Chicago.

Michelle married Barack Obama on October 18, 1992. Their wedding ceremony was performed by Rev. Jeremiah A. Wright, Jr. at Trinity United Church of Christ in Chicago, Illinois.

In 1993, she turned her attention to the non-profit sector and became the founding Executive Director of Public Allies Chicago, an Americorps National Service Program. It was a non-profit organization encouraging young people to work on social issues in non-profit groups and government agencies. Barack Obama was on the founding board of Public Allies, and it was he who recommended his new wife for the job as the Chicago Chapter's first Executive Director, recalled Paul Schmitz, the current president of the group, which is now headquartered in Milwaukee and has chapters in many cities.

The Obama Family Christmas card photo for 2006.

Those who worked for her at Public Allies recall how she challenged them to step outside their zones of comfort, especially those of class and race.

"The most powerful thing she ever taught me was to be constantly aware of my privilege," said Beth Hester, a former staffer. Hester, who is white, said Obama helped her overcome her tendency to avoid difficult situations with people of different races of cultures. "Michelle reminded me that it's too easy to go and sit with your own," Hester said. "She can invite you in kind of an aggressive way to be all you can be."

Through her work with Public Allies in Chicago, Michelle provided internship opportunities and leadership training to hundreds of young adults, ages eighteen to thirty, who were interested in pursuing careers in the public sector. The program provides forty participants with a ten-month apprenticeship opportunity working in a not-for-profit organization or government agency in Chicago.

In 1996, after three years with Public Allies, Michelle was recruited away by the University of Chicago to launch a similar volunteer program based at the Hyde Park High School. In September, she was appointed as the Associate Dean of Student Services and she developed the University's first community service program. She coordinated the University's efforts to make available to students a wide range of service opportunities in the communities around the University as well as throughout the city.

"Michelle understands the Hyde Park community and the world of public service, and her extensive experience in these areas will support and enhance the current efforts by students in these areas," said Arthur Sussman, General Counsel and Vice President for Administration. "She will help our students continue the range of work that has made volunteerism one of the most important extracurricular activities on campus."

Michelle's hiring was a result of recommendations made by the Faculty-Student Committee on Volunteerism, chaired by Harold Richman, then Director of the Chapin Hall Center for Children and the Hermon Dunlop Smith Professor in the School of Social Service Administration. The committee was itself a response to students' widespread interest in volunteer opportunities and community service and the extensive work in these areas by the student-run University Community Service Center.

In 1999, almost seven years after they married, Michelle and Barack's first daughter was born, Malia Ann Obama, with Natasha (often called "Sasha") following two years later in 2001.

In 2002, Michelle came to the University Of Chicago Hospitals and quickly built up programs for community relations, neighborhood outreach, volunteer recruitment, staff diversity and minority contracting. She served as Executive Director of Community and External Affairs.

In 2004, when her husband Barack, then an Illinois state senator, ran for the United States Senate, Michelle's professional relationships were helpful where he faced a primary dominated by some of the Democratic Party's most powerful political families. Barack had the support of influential black business leaders, some of whom had closer ties to Michelle than they did to him. According to *Newsweek*, a former boss of Michelle Obama's, a powerful black woman Valerie Jarrett, chair of the Chicago Stock Exchange, served as finance chair of Barack Obama's U.S. Senate campaign.

After Barack was elected to the U.S. Senate, Barack and Michelle chose to keep their children in Chicago, where Michelle continued her career as well. "We made a good decision to stay in Chicago so that has kept our family stable," Michelle Obama told the *Chicago Tribune*.

According to reports, Michelle has mastered being a mother, career woman and the wife of a politician. When *Newsweek* magazine trailed her in 2004, the reporter could not help but notice a to-do list for her two daughters Malia and Natasha that included time for "play." She is in bed most nights by 9:30 and rises each morning at 4:30 to run on a treadmill. This level of discipline and organization helps her manage her public and private pressures with poise. In *New Yorker* magazine, Michelle noted that the life of a political wife is "hard and that's why Barack is such a grateful man." But there's more to it. "Barack didn't pledge riches," Michelle explains to *Newsweek*, "only a life that would be interesting. On that promise he's delivered."

In March 2005, two months after her husband took office in the U.S. Senate, Michelle was promoted to Vice President of Community and External Affairs at the University Of Chicago Medical Center. Jarrett said Michelle was repeatedly offered the promotion which more than doubled her salary from the hospital.

"We have been impressed with the care, imagination and energy that Michelle has brought to every project she has worked on since coming to the Hospitals," said Michael Riordan, President and CEO of the Hospitals. "We are excited to have her join the ranks of senior management. She brings to our team a new level of compassion, commitment and close connections to the community."

"My goal in this position," Michelle said, "is to continue to broaden the Hospitals' relationships with our neighborhood and with our city." The University Of Chicago Hospitals is one of the largest employers on the South Side and one of the most renowned medical institutions in Chicago and even the Midwest.

Scott Olson/Getty Images

Obama with Sasha at the Iowa State Fair in Aug. 2007

"We have an obligation," she said, "to ensure that we use our resources on behalf of our neighborhood and our city. In this new role, my goal is to better integrate community engagement into the culture of this institution and to expand our partnerships with local organizations and institutions.

A Harvard-trained lawyer, she had steered away from a potentially more lucrative career in private practice. Friends thought her salary was paltry compared to what she could command at a top law firm. But her wages later became public when her husband began his political career. And as his career began to take off, so did scrutiny of their household income. It rose right along with his political career.

The salary questions struck Michelle as sexist and unfair. "I'm a vice president at an academic medical center," she said. "Barack and I have built a joint life together that consists of having two strong individual people who have built careers. Barack hasn't relied deeply on me for his career path, and I haven't relied on him at all for mine. I understand why people want to make sure that somehow I'm not using my husband's influence to build my career. And I haven't."

Hospital officials say the salary was in line with compensation received by the medical center's sixteen other vice presidents, more than a dozen of whom earned in excess of $300,000. She also earned about twenty-five percent less than her counterpart at Northwestern Memorial Hospital.

"My concern was that somebody was going to recruit her," said former U. of C. Hospital's President Michael Riordan.

Losing Michelle Obama, he said, would have been a damaging blow. For all its national prestige, the University Of Chicago Medical Center had a local public-relations problem.

The academic center was spending millions of dollars on care that would have been more effectively dispensed by a primary care provider. It was a dicey issue because it put the prestigious hospital in the position of telling its low-income, underinsured and mostly African-American neighbors to go somewhere else.

Michelle was charged with tackling the problem, a delicate issue not just for her but potentially for her husband. A close ally and supporter of Barack Obama, the Service Employees International Union has been one of the hospital industry's fiercest critics of how it handles care for the uninsured. But the U. of C. program has won praise from community health providers who say Michelle was uniquely suited to tackle the issue.

"Because she is of color, that gives her some credibility," said Wendy Cox, chief executive of Chicago Family Health Center, which operates health centers in the south and southeast sides of the city.

In early 2005, Michelle assembled a meeting of health-care providers and members of the community to ask for their help. She talked about the black community's distrust of the health-care system and about how the lack of health insurance prevents people from seeking less expensive, preventive care.

Bernice Mills, Executive Director of Clinic Operator of Near North Health Service Corp., said the meeting differed markedly from many she had with University of Chicago Hospital executives over the years.

"Her meetings stood out from others because our goals were also her goals," said Mills-Thomas.

The team got to work. Michelle started a screening system to search for people who didn't belong in the ER waiting room. People routinely showed up with lunch and camped out to wait for a doctor. After treating those individuals, hospital employees would sit down and talk with them. Rather than tell them they should go somewhere else in the future, Michelle's staff referred them to specific clinic doctors and scheduled appointments.

Coming from someone else, the message might have inflamed relations with the community. But Michelle spoke as the parent of an asthmatic child, one who knew firsthand the importance of actively managing care. When she was a child growing up not far from the hospital, she recalled, family members would simply wait until they got really sick and then go to the best ER they could find. "It's the most ineffective way to provide care," she said "And it's the most expensive."

After just a year, the effects of the outreach program don't show up in the hospital's bottom line. Still, officials think they're starting to chip away at one of the worst recurring problems of the health system. In the portrait activists often paint to illustrate the problem, the uninsured patients are the victims of the system. While Michelle agrees with that, she also places personal responsibility on the individuals.

"It's a mutual responsibility," she explained in the interview. "Whatever health-care solutions bring to the table, people have to use it. People have to put good food in their bodies. People have to take their medication as directed. People can't sit and completely blame outside forces."

It's a perspective reflected in her husband's viewpoint on health care and other issues. "This is how he thinks about the problems that we face," she said. "You can't just talk about improving education without talking about improving pay for teachers or making sure that parents are doing their part. People have to change their behavior in addition to systems and institutions changing."

Not long after Barack Obama entered the U.S. Senate, Michelle was offered a position on the board of Tree House Foods, a Westchester-based maker of specialty foods. In 2006, the company paid her $51,200 for her board activities, according to the Obama's filed federal income tax return. Factoring in stock options and their payments, the value of her compensation package for serving on the Tree House board last year was $101,083, a recent filing with the Securities and Exchange Commission shows.

On February 10, 2007, United States Senator Barack Obama formally entered the 2008 Democratic race for the presidency, contending he has the experience to know that "Washington must change" and billing himself as the leader who will bring a new generational attitude to address the nation's challenges.

Michelle is more than just a spokeswoman for Barack, she is known for telling it like it is. She's a crucial part of the Obama package itself, complementing and shaping her husband in ways that are both politically and personally significant.

The daughter of a tight-knit nuclear family, she's an anchor for a spouse who grew up all over the world and barely knew his own father. Her background, deeply rooted in a working-class South Side Chicago neighborhood, lends credibility to her husband, who has consistently battled questions from some African-Americans about whether the son of an African father and a white American mother is authentically black. Michelle has listened to that talk many times before, even directed at her.

"I heard that growing up, 'You talk like a white girl'," Michelle told the *Tribune* in her first solo interview since her husband announced his candidacy for president. "There isn't one black person who doesn't understand that dynamic. That debate is about the pain that we still struggle with in this country, and Barack knows that more than anyone."

"One of the things I hope happens through our involvement in this campaign is that this country and this world sees yet another image of what it means to be black."

Her ability to speak with authority on such tough issues is one reason the campaign thinks she will be a potent weapon in its arsenal. In modern politics, the marriage partnership is integral to the quest for the presidency, as voters evaluate a candidate in light of the relationship with his or her spouse.

"She's tough," Barack, said of his wife after she spoke at a luncheon that launched a new group, Women for Obama. "There's something about her that projects such honesty and strength. It's what makes her such an unbelievable professional, and partner, and mother, and wife."

Her career, however, can cause him political discomfort. Tree House, a food company which packages pickles and other private-label foods for retailers, supplies Wal-Mart, who is by far its largest customer. Barack Obama has been sharply critical of Wal-Mart's business and

Michelle Obama by her husband's side after his presidential announcement

Malia and Sasha Obama at their dad's Feb. 2007 presidential announcement.

labor practices-criticizing the giant retailer last fall for paying low wages and poor benefits while making big profits. Michelle, who held a position on the board of Tree House, cut ties immediately after Barack uttered comments critical of Wal-Mart at an AFL-CIO forum in Trenton, New Jersey, on May 14, 2007.

Also, Michelle Obama, as a vice president of The University of Chicago Medical Center, is responsible for guiding low-income patients away from the emergency room and into primary care elsewhere. While South Side activists, as well as Barack, praise her program, Barack's unit on supporters have been critical of the management of many large hospitals for how they deal with charity care for the poor.

Nonetheless, Barack Obama and his campaign are certain Michelle will prove a key asset in his drive for the White House. She has been gearing up her new campaign role, with a new chief of staff, assistant and spokeswoman who have come on board since early March 2007.

Americans are about to see much more of her and the independent style she says her husband admires. "He's one of the few men I've met who is not intimidated by strong women," she said. "He relishes the fact that I'm not impressed by him."

During a period when he was in the Illinois Senate, his wife made no secret of the fact that, too often, he didn't seem to be thinking of this family as much as he thought of himself. In his book *The Audacity of Hope*, he wrote that she would tell him: "I never thought I'd have to raise a family alone."

Michelle Obama's message was not reserved for her husband. She unflinchingly pushed back against political aides she felt were intruding too much on family time, especially where it concerned daughters Malia and Sasha.

"She is as strong and stubborn as he is," said Dan Shomon, and aide to Barack Obama during his unsuccessful challenge against U. S. Rep. Bobby Rush (D-Ill.). "Barack was stuck in Springfield quite a bit in 1999. Because of overtime special sessions, we had to call Michelle and ask her to go to events. She would help if she could, but her family came first."

If Michelle's expectations are hard to live up to, friends think they're also very influential in her husband's understanding of the role of the family in society. He made news on Father's Day, 2005 when, speaking to a mostly black audience, he said that men need to take more responsibility for the care of their children.

"There's a big part of his message that is about personal responsibility," said Shomon. "It's that you can't teach kids to learn if the TV's on. You've got to turn the TV off and take personal responsibility, not just at home but in the community and in the world. That comes from Michelle."

Perhaps in no other matter is Michelle Obama more insistent than on the topic of his cigarette smoking. She's passionate about it, partly because both her parents smoked. As children she and her brother Craig pulled the tobacco out of their parents' cigarettes and doused them with hot sauce.

With her husband, she has been unrelenting in getting him to stop altogether, for his own health and as a good example for Malia, who has asthma. Michelle said he has never smoked in the presence of her or their girls. Her support for his presidential bid came with a special contingency clause: no cigarettes. And he announced he had quit just days before declaring his candidacy. “To me it’s a role model thing,” she said. “You can smoke or you can be president.”

In May 2006, *Essence* magazine listed her among "25 of the World's Most Inspiring Women” and in July 2007, *Vanity Fair* magazine listed her among "10 of the World's Best Dressed People."

In 2007, Michelle gave political stump speeches for her husband at various locations in the United States. Jennifer Hunter of the *Chicago Sun Times* wrote about one speech of hers in Iowa: "Michelle was a firebrand, expressing a determined passion for her husband's campaign, talking straight from the heart with eloquence and intelligence."

Michelle Obama serves on a variety of boards and commissions including the board of the Otho S.A. Sprague Memorial Institute, Facing History and Ourselves, and the Muntu Dance Company. She is also a former member of the Commission on Chicago Landmarks.

CHAPTER 4 – SHIRLEY CHISHOLM

Shirley Anita St. Hill Chisholm became the first African American woman candidate to seek the nomination of the Democratic Party for President of the United States on January 25, 1972. Chisholm received about ten percent of the vote at the party's national convention. She lost the nomination to George McGovern.

Shirley Anita St. Hill was born on November 30, 1924, in Brooklyn, New York. Her parents were immigrants, her father Guyanese and her mother Barbadian. She spent part of her childhood in Barbados with her grandmother, and received an education in the British-run school system. She returned to New York when she was ten years old. She attended Girls' High School in Bedford-Stuyvesant, a section of the city with a growing poor black and immigrant population. She won tuition scholarships to both Oberlin and Vassar, but at the urging of her parents decided to live at home and attend Brooklyn College. She graduated with a Bachelor of Arts degree in 1946, majoring in Sociology. In 1948, she married Conrad Chisholm, a Jamaican who worked as a private investigator. Shirley and her husband participated in local politics, helping form the Bedford-Stuyvesant political League. While working as a teacher, Shirley Chisholm earned a Master's degree in elementary education from Teachers College, Columbia University. From 1953 to 1959, she was Director of the Hamilton-Madison Child Care Center, and from 1959 to 1964, she was an educational consultant for the Division of Day Care. In 1960, she started the Unity Democratic Club. The Unity Democratic Club was instrumental in mobilizing black and Hispanic voters.

In 1964, Chisholm ran for a state assembly seat. She won and served in the New York General Assembly from 1964 to 1968. During the time that she served in the assembly, Chisholm sponsored fifty bills, but only eight of them passed. She proposed a bill to provide state aid to day-care centers and voted to increase funding for schools on a per-pupil basis. The bills she sponsored reflected her interest in the cause of blacks and the poor, women's rights, and educational opportunities. One of the successful bills provided assistance for poor students to go on for higher education. Another provided employment insurance coverage for personal and domestic employees. Still another reversed a law that caused female teachers in New York to lose their tenure while they were out on maternity leave.

After finishing her term in the legislature, Chisholm ran as the Democratic candidate for New York's 12th District congressional seat. Her campaign slogan was "Fighting Shirley Chisholm--Unbought and Unbossed." She was elected to the House of Representatives in 1968, defeating Republican candidate James Farmer and becoming the first African-American woman elected to Congress. Possibly because Chisholm was a well-known resident of Bedford-Stuyvesant and Farmer was not, she won easily. Thus began her tenure in the U.S. House of Representatives from the 91st through the 97th Congress (1969-1982).

Chisholm served on several House committees: Agriculture, Veterans' Affairs, Rules and Education, and Labor. Always considering herself a political maverick, Chisholm attempted to focus as much of her attention as possible on the needs of her constituents. During the 91st Congress she was assigned to the Forestry Subcommittee of the Agricultural Committee. She felt the placement was a waste of time given her urban district and shocked many by demanding reassignment. She wanted to work on committees that could deal with the "critical problems of racism, deprivation and urban decay."

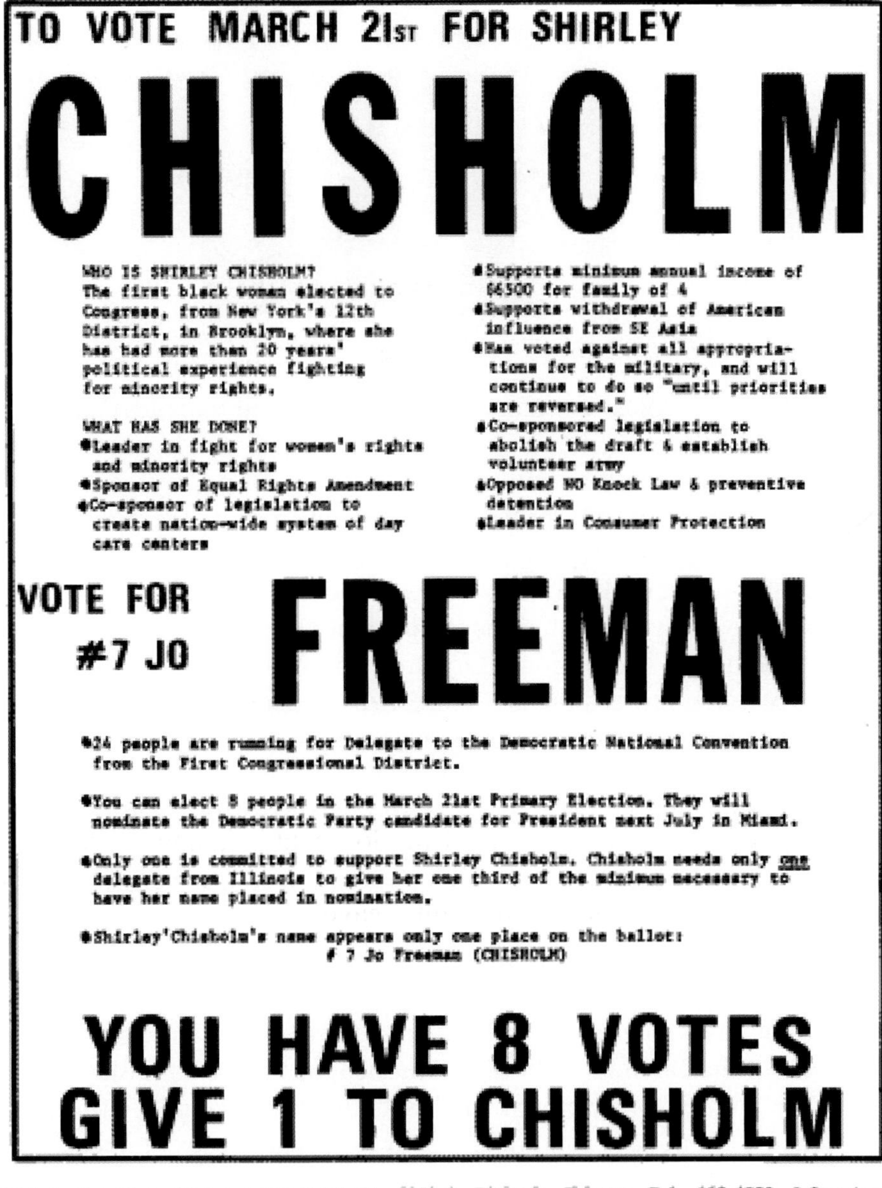

A campaign poster for Shirley Chisholm's Presidential race.

A man shows his support for Shirley Chisholm's Presidential run.

Chisholm began to protest the amount of money being expended for the defense budget while social programs suffered. She argued that she would not agree that money should be spent for war while Americans were hungry, ill-housed, and poorly educated. Chisholm hired an all-female staff and spoke out for civil rights, women's rights, the poor and against the Vietnam War. She began to support legislation allowing abortions for women who chose to have them. Her antiwar and women's liberation views made her a popular figure among college students, and she was besieged with invitations to speak at college campuses.

Chisholm co-founded the National Organization for Women (NOW). She protested the traditional roles for women professionals - secretaries, teachers, and librarians. She argued that women were capable of entering many other professions and they should be encouraged to do so. Black women, too, she felt, had been shunted into stereotypical maid and nanny roles from which they needed to escape both by legislation and by self-effort. She remarked that, "Women in this country must become revolutionaries. We must refuse to accept the old, the traditional roles and stereotypes." Chisholm joined the Congressional Black Caucus in 1969, as one of its founding members.

On January 25, 1972, Chisholm announced her candidacy for Democratic Party's presidential nomination. She stood before the cameras and in the beginning of her speech she said, "I stand before you today as a candidate for the Democratic nomination for the Presidency of the United States. I am not the candidate of black America, although I am black and proud. I am not the candidate of the women's movement of this country, although I am a woman, and I am equally proud of that. I am not the candidate of any political bosses or special interests. I am the candidate of the people."

Shirley Chisholm address at the DNC.

Chisholm supporter at the DNC.

She received 152 delegate votes, but ultimately lost the nomination to South Dakota Senator George McGovern, who was defeated by Republican incumbent Richard Nixon in the general election. Chisholm's base of support was ethnically diverse and included the National Organization for Women. Chisholm said she ran for the office "in spite of hopeless odds, to demonstrate the sheer will and refusal to accept the status quo."

Chisholm created controversy when she visited rival and ideological opposite George Wallace in the hospital soon after his shooting in May 1972, during the 1972 presidential primary campaign. Several years later, when Chisholm worked on a bill to give domestic workers the right to a minimum wage, Wallace got her the votes of enough southern congressmen to push the legislation through the House. Throughout her tenure in Congress, Chisholm would work to improve opportunities for inner-city residents. She was a vocal opponent of the draft and supported spending increases for education, healthcare and other social services, and reductions in military spending.

Chisholm divorced Conrad Chisholm in 1977, and upon their divorce, she married Arthur Hardwick, Jr., who died in 1986. She had no children. She announced her retirement from Congress in 1982, and was replaced by a fellow Democrat, Major Owens, in 1983. After leaving Congress, Chisholm was named to the Purington Chair and she resumed her career in education, teaching politics and women's studies at Mount Holyoke College in South Hadley, Massachusetts from 1983 to 1987. In 1985, she was a visiting scholar at Spelman College. In 1984 and 1988, she campaigned for Jesse Jackson for the presidential elections. In 1993, then-President Bill Clinton nominated her to the ambassadorship to Jamaica, but she could not serve due to poor health. In the same year she was inducted into the National Women's Hall of Fame.

Shirley Chisholm was a member of Delta Sigma Theta Sorority. Chisholm also authored two books, *Unbought and Unbossed* (1970) and *The Good Fight* (1973). Chisholm retired to Ormond Beach, Florida and died on January 1, 2005. She is buried in Forest Lawn Cemetery in Buffalo, NY.

Political buttons for Chisholm's campaign for president.

Shirley Chisholm being buried.

CHAPTER FIVE - DICK GREGORY

Dick Gregory in 1964

Richard Claxton Gregory was born October 12, 1932, and is an American comedian, social activist, writer and entrepreneur. Born in St. Louis, Missouri, United States, Dick Gregory is an influential African American comic who has used his performance skills to convey to both white and black audiences his political message on civil rights. Influenced to stand up for civil rights by his early surroundings of poverty and violence, Gregory became the first comedian to successfully perform for both black and white audiences.

As a poor student who excelled at running, Gregory was aided by high school teachers at Summer High such as Warren St. James and earned a track scholarship to Southern Illinois University, Carbondale. There he set records as a half-miler and miler. His college career was interrupted by two years in the U.S. Army where he got his start in comedy, entering and winning several Army talent shows at the urging of his commanding officer.

The office had taken notice of his penchant for joking. After completing military service, he performed as a comedian in small, primarily black nightclubs while working for the United States Postal Service during the daytime. Dick Gregory entered the national comedy scene in 1961, while working at the Black-owned Roberts Show Bar in Chicago. Due to a direct request from publisher Hugh Hefner, Gregory was hired to work at the Chicago Playboy Club after Hefner heard him wow a largely-white audience. Before then he had worked mostly at small clubs with predominantly black audiences. He met his wife Lillian while performing at one club.

He soon began appearing nationally and on television and his 1964 autobiography, *Nigger,* sold seven million copies. At the same time, he became more involved in struggles for civil rights, activism against the American War in Vietnam, economic reform, anti-drug issues, conspiracy theories, and others. As a part of his activism, he went on several hunger strikes. Gregory began his political career by running against Richard Daley for the mayoralty of Chicago in 1967. Though he did not emerge victorious, this would not prove to be the end of Dick Gregory's dalliances with electoral politics.

1968 Presidential Campaign

Gregory unsuccessfully ran for president of the United States in 1968 as a write-in candidate of the Freedom and Peace Party, which had broken off from the Peace and Freedom Party. He won 47,097 votes with fellow activist Mark Lane as his running mate, garnering more than the party he had left.

The Peace and Freedom Party's first national convention to nominate candidates for President and Vice President was held in Ann Arbor, Michigan on August 17-August 18, 1968. Eldridge Cleaver was nominated for President over Richard C. "Dick" Gregory by a margin of 161.5 to fifty-four. This is when Gregory formed a competing Freedom and Peace Party and ran separately. Two states (California and Utah) refused to list Cleaver on the ballot, although each state listed the Presidential Electors and candidates for Vice President (Terry in California and Gonzalez in Utah).

In the election of 1968, the PFP fared fairly well for a new third party. Gregory outpolled Cleaver, receiving 47,097 votes to Cleaver's 36,623. In California and Utah, where no presidential nominee appeared on the ballot, the voters cast 27,887 votes for the PFP. The full nationwide vote for Presidential Electors was thus 111,607. PFP candidates for the U.S. Senate garnered an aggregate nationwide total of 105,411 votes.

The Freedom and Peace Party also ran other candidates, including Beulah Sanders for New York State Senate and Flora Brown for New York State Assembly. His efforts landed him on the master list of Nixon political opponents.

He then wrote "Write Me In," about his presidential campaign. One interesting anecdote in the book related the story of a publicity stunt which came out of Operation Breadbasket in Chicago where the campaign had printed hundred dollar bills with Gregory's image on them. Some of these bills made it into circulation in cash transactions causing considerable problems, but priceless publicity.

As of 2005, "Dick and "Lil" have ten children, and one child who died during childbirth. They have shared forty-two years of selfless dedication and tremendous personal love.

DICK GREGORY

A pioneer of the new black comedy, Gregory often lectured at colleges where he applied his bitter irony to the crusade for black rights.

CHAPTER SIX – JESSE LOUIS JACKSON

Jesse Jackson, July 1, 1983

Jesse Louis Jackson was born on October 8, 1941, in Greenville, South Carolina, the son of Noah Louis Robinson and Helen Burns. Two years after Jesse's birth, his mother married Charles Henry Jackson and he was adopted by his stepfather. Jesse went on to take the surname of his step-father.

Jackson attended Sterling High School, a segregated high school in Greenville, where he was an outstanding student athlete. Upon graduating in 1959, he rejected a contract from a professional baseball team to attend the racially integrated University of Illinois on a football scholarship. However, one year later, Jackson transferred to North Carolina Agricultural and Technical State University (A&T) located in Greensboro. Differing accounts exist for the reasons behind this transfer. Jackson claims that the change was based on the school's racial biases which included Jackson being unable to play as a quarterback (despite being a star quarterback at his high school) as well as being demoted by his speech professor as an alternate in a public speaking competition team, despite the support of his teammates who elected him a place on the team for his superior abilities. Entertainment and Sports Programming Network reported a different story on their website, ESPN.com. Claims of racial discrimination on the football team may be exaggerated because Illinois' starting quarterback that year was an African American. In addition, Jackson left Illinois at the end of his second semester after being placed on academic probation. Following his graduation from A&T, Jackson attended the Chicago Theological Seminary with the intent of becoming a minister, but dropped out in 1966 to focus full-time on the civil rights movement.

In 1965, Jesse Jackson participated in Martin Luther King, Jr.'s movement in Selma, Alabama. When Jackson returned from Selma, he threw himself into King's effort to establish a beachhead of the Southern Christian Leadership Conference (SCLC) in Chicago. In 1966, King selected Jackson to be head of the SCLC's Operation Breadbasket in Chicago, and promoted him to be the national director in 1967. Following the example of Reverend Leon Sullivan of Philadelphia, a key goal of the new group was to foster "selective buying" (boycotts) as a means to pressure white businesses to hire blacks and purchase goods and services from black contractors. One of Sullivan's precursors was Dr. T.R.M. Howard, a wealthy South Side doctor and entrepreneur and key financial contributor to Operation Breadbasket. Before he moved to Chicago from Mississippi in 1956, Howard, as the head of the Regional Council of Negro Leadership, had successfully organized a boycott against service stations that refused to provide restrooms for blacks.

Jackson was present with King in Memphis when he was assassinated on April 4, 1968, the day after making his famous "I've Been to the Mountaintop" speech given to the Mason Temple, Church of God in Christ.

Beginning in 1968, Jackson increasingly clashed with Ralph Abernathy, King's successor as head of the national SCLC. In December, 1971, they had a complete falling out. Abernathy suspended Jackson for "administrative improprieties and repeated acts of violation of organizational policy." Jackson resigned, called together his allies, and Operation PUSH was born during the same month. The new group was organized in the home of Dr. T.R.M. Howard, who also became a member of the board of directors and chair of the finance committee.

In 1984, Jackson organized the Rainbow Coalition, which later merged, in 1996, with Operation PUSH. The newly formed Rainbow PUSH organization brought the reverend's role as an important and effective organizer to the mainstream.

That same year, Jackson became the second African American (after Shirley Chisholm) to mount a nationwide campaign for President of the United States, running as a Democrat.

In the primaries, Jackson, who had been written off by pundits as a fringe candidate with little chance at winning the nomination, surprised many when he took third place behind Senator Gary Hart and former Vice President Walter Mondale, who eventually won the nomination. Jackson garnered 3.5 million votes and won five primaries, including Michigan.

As he had gained twenty-one percent of the popular vote but only eight-percent of delegates, he afterwards complained that he had been handicapped by party rules. While Mondale (in the words of his aides) was determined to establish a precedent with his vice presidential candidate by picking a woman or visible minority, Jackson criticized the screening process as a

"P.R. parade of personalities." He also mocked Mondale, saying that Hubert Humphrey was the "last significant politician out of the St. Paul-Minneapolis" area.

Four years later, in 1988, Jackson once again offered himself as a candidate for the Democratic Party presidential nomination. This time, his successes in the past made him a more credible candidate, and he was both better financed and better organized. Although most people did not seem to believe that he had a serious chance at winning, Jackson once again exceeded expectations as he more than doubled his previous results, capturing 6.9 million votes and winning eleven primaries. Briefly, after he won fifty-five percent of the vote in the Michigan Democrat caucus, he was considered the frontrunner for the nomination, as he surpassed all the other candidates in total number of pledged delegates.

In early 1988, Jackson organized a rally at the former American Motors assembly plant in Kenosha, Wisconsin approximately two weeks after the new owner, Chrysler, announced the plant would close by the end of the year. In his speech, Jackson spoke out against Chrysler's decision, stating "We have to put the focus on Kenosha, Wisconsin, as the place, here and now, where we draw the line to end economic violence!" and compared the workers' fight to that of the civil rights movement in Selma, Alabama. As a result, the UAW Local 72 union voted to endorse his candidacy, even against the rules of the UAW. However, Jackson's campaign suffered a significant setback less than two weeks later when he was defeated handily in the Wisconsin primary be Michael Dukakis. Jackson's showing among white voters in Wisconsin was significantly higher than in his 1984 run, but was also noticeably lower than pre-primary polling had indicated it would be. The discrepancy has been cited as an example of the so called "Bradley effect."

Jackson's run had also been interrupted by an ill-timed event involving his half-brother Noah Robinson, Jr. During Jesse Jackson's campaign he had to answer frequent questions about his brother, who was often referred to as "the Billy Carter of the Jackson campaign."

On the heels of Jackson's narrow loss to Dukakis the day before in Colorado, Dukakis' comfortable win in Wisconsin terminated Jackson's momentum. The victory established Dukakis as the clear Democratic frontrunner, and he went on to claim the party's nomination.

In both races, Jackson ran on what many considered to be a very liberal platform. Declaring that he wanted to create a "Rainbow Coalition" of various minority groups, including African-Americans, Hispanics, Arab-Americans, Asian Americans, Native Americans, family farmers, the poor and working class, and homosexuals, as well as white progressives who fit into none of those categories, Jackson ran on a platform that included:

1. Creating a Works Progress Administration–style program to rebuild America's infrastructure and provide jobs to all Americans.
2. Reprioritizing the war on Drugs to focus less on mandatory minimum sentences for drug users (which he views as racially biased) and more on harsher punishments for money-laundering bankers and others who are part of the "supply" end of "supply and demand."

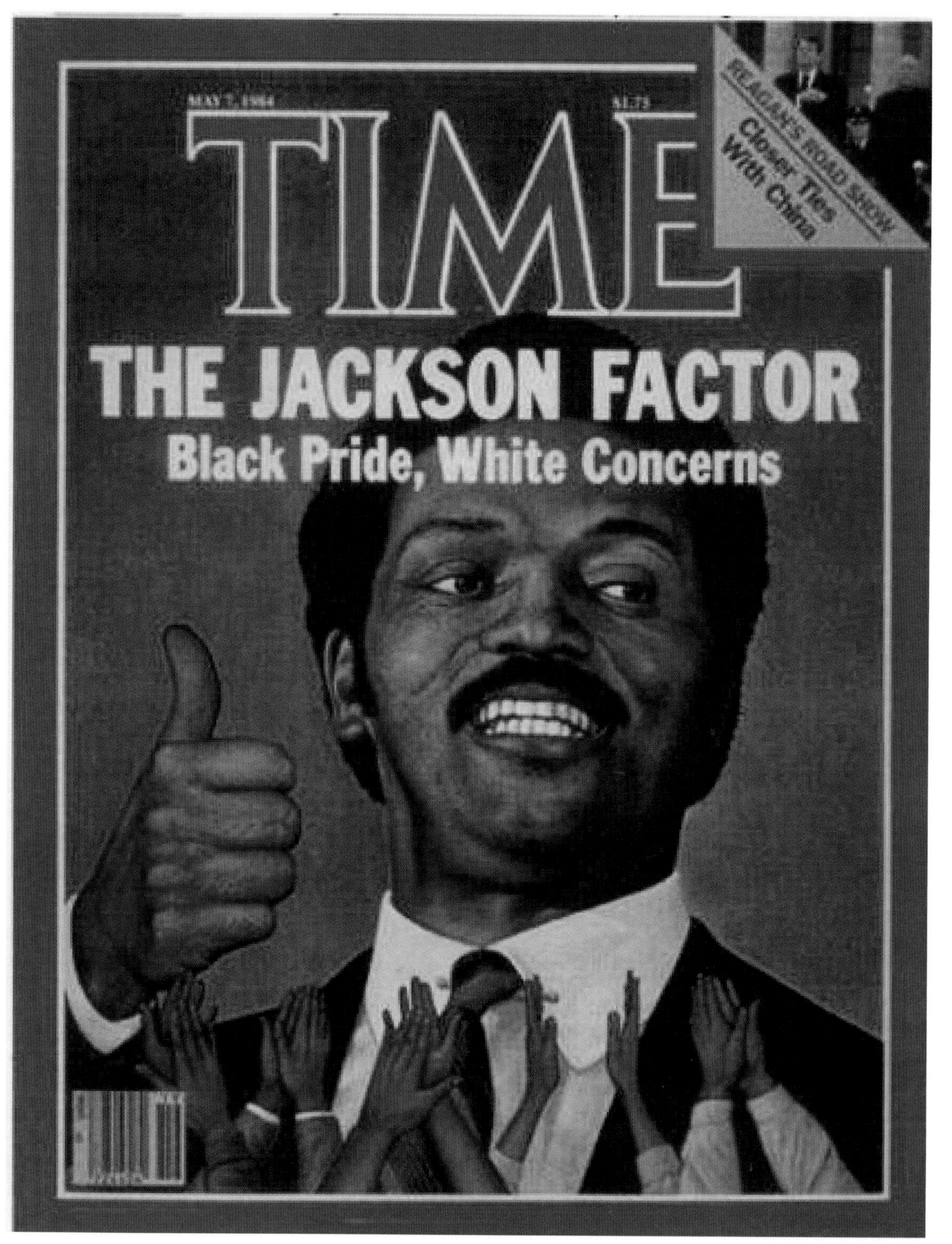

TIME Magazine Cover, May 7, 1984

Rev. Jackson gives an emotional speech at the DNC in Atlanta, July 18, 1988.

3. Cutting the budget of the Department of defense by as much as fifteen percent over the course of his administration.
4. Declaring Apartheid-era South Africa to be a rogue nation.
5. Instituting an immediate nuclear freeze and beginning disarmament negotiations with the Soviet Union.
6. Giving reparations to descendants of black slaves.
7. Supporting family farmers by reviving many of Roosevelt's New Deal-era farm programs.
8. Creating a single-payer system of universal health care.
9. Ratifying the Equal Rights Amendment.
10. Increasing federal funding for lower-level public education and providing free community college to all.
11. Applying stricter enforcement of the Voting Rights Act,.
12. Supporting the formation of a Palestinian state.

With the exception of a resolution to implement sanctions against South Africa for its Apartheid policies, none of these positions made it into the party's platform in either 1984 or 1988.

Jesse Jackson and his wife, Jaqueline Lavinia (Brown) Jackson, have been married since 1962. They have three sons and two daughters, and Jesse has another daughter with Karin Stanford.

CHAPTER 7 – CAROL MOSELEY BRAUN

Carol Elizabeth Moseley Braun announced on February 19, 2003, that she would run as a candidate for the Democratic Party nomination in the 2004 U.S. Presidential Election. On January 15, 2004, she dropped out of the race for the White House and endorsed Howard Dean.

Carol Elizabeth Moseley was born on August 16, 1947, to a middle-class family in a segregated neighborhood on the South Side of Chicago, Illinois. Her father was a Chicago Police Officer and musician and her mother was a medical technician. She grew up in Chicago and was educated in Chicago Public Schools. Instilled with a strong sense of community interest and commitment to racial justice, a teenaged Braun staged a one-person sit-in at a restaurant that would not serve her, withstood the stone-throwing of whites when she refused to leave an all-white beach, and at sixteen, marched alongside Martin Luther King, Jr. in an open-housing demonstration in an all-white neighborhood.

Moseley earned her Bachelor of Arts degree majoring in Political Science from the University of Illinois at Chicago in 1969. She went on to the University Of Chicago Law School, where she was awarded her Doctor of Jurisprudence degree in 1972. While still in law school, she began her legal career as a law clerk with Mayer, Brown, and Platt (1970) and Rose, Hardies, O'Keefe, Babcock, and Parsons (1971). After earning her Doctorate, she spent one year as an associate with the firm of Davis, Miner, and Barnhill. In 1973, she was admitted to the Illinois Bar and also married Michael Braun.

In 1973, Moseley-Braun was appointed Assistant U.S. Attorney for the Northern District of Illinois, under future Governor of Illinois Jim Thompson, and his deputy, Samuel Skinner. As an Assistant United States Attorney, she worked primarily in the civil and appellate law areas. Her work in housing, health policy, and environmental law won her the Attorney General's Special Achievement Award. She subsequently received over 300 awards for achievements in the public interest. She left the US Attorney's office in 1977 to start a family, giving birth to her only son, Matthew.

In 1978, she sought and won election to the Illinois House of Representatives in Springfield. She fought for reform in education, welfare, health care, and gun control. She proposed a moratorium on the application in Illinois of the death penalty. And in what became a landmark reapportionment case, Crosby vs. State Board of Elections, she successfully sued her own party and the state of Illinois on behalf of African American and Hispanic citizens. She was the Chief sponsor of the 1985 Urban School Improvement Act which created and empowered parents' councils at every school in Chicago. She was the chief sponsor and prime mover of every school funding bill that affected education in the City of Chicago from 1980-87.

Other education legislation sponsored by Moseley-Braun included a bill, introduced in 1980, that provided for higher salaries for professors and a bill, passed in 1984, which allows public aid recipients to attend college without losing their benefits.

After just two terms in the Illinois House, Moseley-Braun rose to the position of Assistant Majority Leader, becoming the first African American and the first woman to do so. She had earned a reputation as a dynamic debater and an uncompromising advocate for more efficient and accountable government. Her hallmark has been an ability to build coalitions comprised of people of all races who are committed to the same principles of good government. For each of her ten years in the legislature, Carol Moseley-Braun received the "Best Legislator" award given by the Independent Voters of Illinois - Independent Precinct Organization (IVI-IPO).

In 1983, Harold Washington, the first black mayor of Chicago, named Braun his floor leader in the legislature, even though she was not the senior legislator from the city. She was the chief sponsor of bills to reform education and to ban discrimination in housing and private clubs. She also introduced the bill that barred the State of Illinois from investing funds in South Africa until the apartheid system was abolished. Moseley-Braun filed, and won, the reapportionment case which affirmed the "one man - one vote" principle in Illinois. But her unflinching independence, evidenced in her reluctance to follow Washington unquestioningly, reportedly led to his blocking a 1986 recruitment of her to run as the state's Lieutenant Governor.

Also in 1986, she reached her lowest emotional point. Her marriage ended in divorce, her brother died from a drug and alcohol overdose, and her mother suffered a debilitating stroke.

In 1988, she was elected Cook County Recorder of Deeds, Registrar of Titles with more than one million votes cast in her favor. She was also the first woman and first African American elected to an executive in Cook County. Running an office with 300 employees and an $8 million budget, Braun was credited with streamlining the agency through computerization and eliminating political patronage through the implementation of a code of ethics.

Moseley-Braun entered the Illinois Senate Primary Race. The little publicity she got revolved around her grass-roots campaign, which was beset by resignations, disorganization, and charges of mismanagement. She also got little help from her fellow politicians, garnering the support of only two members of the Illinois congressional delegation. Despite fund-raising help from feminist Gloria Steinem, her candidacy appeared so unpromising that political organizations created to provide seed money to women's campaigns across the country gave her nothing or just token contributions late in the race.

During the campaign, her opponents, Alfred Hofeld, a multimillionaire personal injury and products-liability lawyer and a political newcomer, spent roughly $5 million on advertisements trashing Illinois Senator Alan J. Dixon as the archetypal incumbent, an entrenched senator out of touch with his constituency and in the pockets of special interest groups. Dixon, who had never lost an election in his forty-three year political career and was the champion

Braun's official Senate portrait.

vote-getter in state history, retaliated by dishing out $2 million for ads defending himself and targeting Hofeld. Braun was untouched in the fray. It was this invisibility and low-key profile that political observers say were Braun's most valuable assets. By not participating in the negative advertisements, the defining feature of many modern campaigns, Braun emerged looking the least political and--in this period of anti-politics--the most attractive of all the candidates.

Despite spending only $350,000 on the campaign--she could only afford two television advertisements, which ran one week before the election, Braun's win upset two-term Democratic incumbent Dixon after the votes were counted. The final tally had Braun at thirty-eight percent, Dixon at thirty-five, and Hofeld at twenty-seven. Her victory was helped by votes she received from crossover white Republican women.

Moseley-Braun ran against Republican Richard S. Williamson, a one-time Assistant Secretary of State in the Ronald Reagan White House. Braun voiced her support for a personal income tax increase on the top one percent of wage-earners, $100 billion worth of cuts in defense spending, a capital gains tax cut (which would decrease taxes on the increased value of investments), and a universal health care plan. "It's a historic candidacy and we're looking to make history," she told the *Boston Globe*. "The state is ready and willing to strike a blow for revitalizing our democracy and opening the doors to the Senate."

Several scandals had eroded the huge lead Braun had carried over from her primary victory. The most taxing political crisis came when a local television station reported that Braun had mishandled a $28,750 royalty payment made to her mother on timber sales from family-owned land in Alabama. Williamson capitalized on the controversy, accusing Braun of lacking integrity because the money had not been turned over to the state, as required by law, to determine if it should be used to help pay Edna Moseley's nursing home bills, which were being funded by Medicaid. Braun admitted to mishandling the money, and her favorability ratings dropped precipitously. Also dogging her candidacy were concerns leftover from her primary fight--namely that she had not built a disciplined campaign and that she was running on a general anti-incumbency platform rather than on detailed, well-articulated positions.

Williamson failed to present himself as a reasonable, strong alternative, and on November 3, 1992, Braun managed to win a decisive ten-point victory with fifty-three percent of the vote, becoming the first female Senator from Illinois, the first female African-American Senator and the first African-American Democratic Senator. Braun took office on January 5, 1993, to serve the people of Illinois and was named to the Judiciary Committee, the Banking, Housing and Urban Affairs Committee and the Small Business Committee.

Braun worked hard to make her name become connected with positive movements within the Senate and to push for more focus on civil rights and the rights of women, two of the main issues that she had used during her campaign for office. In 1994, she authored the Educational Infrastructure Act, designed to channel education funds into the areas most needed by low-income communities.

By 1995, things seemed to be heading in the right direction for Braun as she was named to the Senate Finance Committee. This was an honor not only because the Finance Committee was one of the most powerful in the Senate, but also because Braun was the first woman to be named to a full term on the Committee. She told *Jet* that she felt she could make a difference by being on this committee because, "The legislation that comes before the Finance Committee affects every American--particularly middle-class Americans, poor Americans, and elderly Americans."

The next two years would be trying times for Braun as she weathered accusation after accusation. When she visited Nigeria in 1996, on a vacation, she was chided by many members of the government for showing support for the authoritarian government run by General Sani Abacha, a man notorious for human rights violations. She was also admonished for not notifying the State Department of her trip to the country, but as she told *Jet*, "I am not a member of the administration, and it is up to the president and his administration to conduct U.S. foreign policy. And I made it clear when I was there that I was on private time, and it was a private trip." There was also question as to what funds were used to pay for this trip and an inquiry was started into Braun's personal and government funds.

Another scandal that rocked her time in office was the Internal Revenue Service (IRS) criminal tax division's investigation of her 1992 campaign as well as her time as the Cook County recorder. The IRS claimed that Braun had used $280,000 that she had raised in political donations for personal expenses including trips to foreign countries, two jeeps, jewelry and clothes. Fortunately for Braun, these charges were never brought to fruition due to Justice Department intercession and a lack of funding in the IRS to keep the investigation going, but the press heavily covered the IRS's claims and the public began to lose trust in Braun.

The Senate Democratic Women in 1993

She received several awards during this time, including the Karunya Educational Award for Legislative Excellence; Business & Professional Women, Magnificent 7 Award in 1996, the Minority Economic Resources Corp, Woman of the Year in 1997 and the Interdenominational Ministerial Alliance of Chicago, Martin Luther King, Jr. Excellence Award in 1997.

However, by the time 1998 rolled around, it was clear that she was going to have a difficult time holding onto her Senate seat. Even though then-President Bill Clinton and first-lady Hillary Clinton supported her, Braun could do little to change the perception of her that was filtering through the public. She focused her campaign around the idea of apologizing for past mistakes and looking forward to a more productive political future. This bolstered little public support. The final blows to her campaign came late in the election when she verbally insulted a conservative columnist with racial slurs and was also found to have her sister selling fund-raiser tickets directly out of her office, which is a campaign law violation. When the election was held in November of 1998, Braun found herself on the losing side by four percent of the vote.

After the election, Braun told *Jet* that she would "never again run for public office." Instead, she decided to focus on education, one of the issues during her time as a senator that meant the most to her. She was approached by the U.S. Department of Education and taken on as a consultant in charge of investigating school construction issues and reporting these to the department's Intergovernmental and Interagency Affairs.

Shortly after this, however, she was approached by the Clinton administration to become an ambassador to New Zealand and Samoa. At first it appeared that Braun would turn them down, for according to the *Chicago Tribune* and reprinted in *Black Issues in Higher Education*, a source close to Braun said, "This job [with the Education Department] keeps her in the country and is temporary in nature while she waits for her other options to gel. I don't think she wanted to go halfway around the world." This source was soon proved incorrect when Braun accepted the appointment. However, her confirmation was held up by the late Senator Jesse Helms, but she was finally sworn in on December 9, 1999.

While her time in New Zealand helped to remove her from much of the critical eye of the American public, it was not without its own controversy. Only ten months after she had arrived in New Zealand, she was involved with allegations that she had accepted free hotel stays as well as other gifts which are ethical violations of the ambassadorial position. Braun was cleared by the Justice Department of all wrong doing, but to many, this was just one more example of Braun's inability to lead without corruption.

She returned in 2001, and accepted a position as a visiting distinguished professor and scholar in residence at Morris Brown College. After a year, she moved on to teach business law at DePaul University's College of Commerce. Many people felt that this was a perfect position for her since she herself had been at the center of many controversial issues revolving around business laws. Braun told *Black Issues in Higher Education* that her purpose in teaching the class was to "recommit to producing leaders who better understand and can better fulfill their responsibilities."

Ambassador Moseley Braun

Braun officially declared her candidacy in a 15-minute speech at Howard University.

On February 19, 2003, Braun filed papers establishing a presidential exploratory committee, allowing her to seek the Democratic presidential nomination in 2004. She made "renewed peace, prosperity and progress for all Americans" the theme of her campaign. She told *Black Enterprise*, "I'm in this race to ensure that the American dream finally gets extended to all Americans without regard to race, color, or gender."

Many of Braun's critics have already pointed to the fact that she was already running a campaign based not on issues but on the fact that she is a minority female. However, according to *Off Our Backs* magazine, "Braun hopes to lead the Democrats to offer a sharper contrast to the policies of the current administration. She has criticized Bush's push for war on Iraq despite the lack of international support and his tax cuts that she says our children will be forced to pay for later." Braun also hoped that voters would look towards her experience as a deciding factor. She told *Black Enterprise*, "I am the only former diplomat in the race and as a former state representative and Cook County recorder of deeds, I'm the only one with both state and local government experience." She told *CNN News,* as reprinted on *America's Intelligence Wire,* "I hope that this campaign will be about the future. That I'll be able to talk about my whole record as well as my standing for human rights, my standing for reform in government, my standing for inclusion. And that's what this campaign is all about, and that's why I'm so excited about it, because it gives me a chance to engage on those issues." She received the endorsements of the National Organization for Women (NOW) and the National Women's Political Caucus which determined her to formally declare her candidacy. She continued a low key campaign over the next months with a modest fundraising of just $217,108.85 in the first two quarters.

Braun could not keep up with the other Democratic candidates and on January 15, 2004, dropped out of the race for the White House and endorsed Howard Dean. Despite Braun's decision to end her run in the presidential race, Ms. President PAC and American Women Presidents, two organizations dedicated to helping women run for the presidency, honored her with the 2004 Ms. President Award. Mosemarie Boyd, who is the spokeswoman for both organizations, told *America's Intelligence Wire,* "[w]omen cannot win the U.S. presidency unless we run for the office and Braun understands that."

Moseley Braun is divorced and resides in Hyde Park, Chicago, Illinois. She currently runs a private law firm, Moseley Braun, L.L.C. in Chicago, Illinois. Moseley Braun has launched a line of organic food products called Ambassador Organics. In April 2007, Braun suffered a broken wrist when a mugger emerged from bushes near her front door to steal her purse, cutting the strap with a knife. Braun resisted and fell during the struggle, fracturing her left wrist. The mugger was chased off without the purse by University of Chicago student Zachary Trayes-Gibson while his girlfriend called 9-1-1. Braun was later treated and released from a hospital. A suspect was later arrested for the incident and has pleaded not guilty.

CHAPTER EIGHT – BOBBY RUSH

The rise of Barack Obama includes one glaring episode of political miscalculation. Even friends told Obama it was a bad idea when he decided in 1999 to challenge an incumbent congressman and former Black Panther, Bobby L. Rush, whose stronghold on the Southside of Chicago was overwhelmingly black, Democratic and working class.

Obama was a thirty-eight year old Harvard Law School graduate and state senator, plus a University of Chicago lecturer, unknown in much of Rush's Congressional District. He lived in the most diversified neighborhood on the Southside, Hyde Park. He was taking on a local legend, a former alderman and four-term controversial incumbent who had given voters no obvious reason to displace him.

Rush's name recognition started off at ninety percent, Obama's at eleven. Then Rush's son was murdered, leaving Obama to put his campaign on hold. Later, while vacationing in Hawaii with his family, he missed a high-profile vote in the Legislature and was pilloried. One *Chicago Tribune* editorial began, "What a bunch of gutless sheep." However, President Clinton endorsed Rush.

"Campaigns are always about 'what's the narrative of the race?'" said Eric Adelstein, a media consultant in Chicago who worked on the Rush campaign. "In a sense, it was 'the Black Panther against the professor.' That's not a knock on Obama, because he came from Hyde Park, a bastion of academia, a white community on the black Southside. It just seemed odd that he would make that choice as a kind of stepping out."

The episode revealed a lot about Senator Obama, now running for president against the odds again and with a relatively slim resume.

It showed his impatience with the frustrations of his state Senate job, his oversized confidence, his fund-raising powers, his broad appeal, and his willingness to be what Abner J. Mikva, a former congressman and supporter calls "a very apt student of his own mistakes."

It also shed light on the complicated ways that class has played out in Obama's political career as a factor entangled with his race. Class emerged as a subtext in the Congressional campaign, along with generational differences that separate Obama from the older black politicians.

People involved in that campaign say he might have fared better if he had jumped into the race sooner, campaigned even harder and found a way to speak more effectively to working class black voters. But most say they doubt he could have won. It is hard to take out an incumbent, and though Rush may have looked vulnerable after losing a lackluster campaign against Mayor Richard M. Daley in early 1999, he was not vulnerable enough.

"He was blinded by his ambition," Rush said. "Obama has never suffered from a lack of believing that he can accomplish whatever it is he decides to try. Obama believes in Obama, and frankly, that has its good side but it also has its negative side."

Not that the loss hurt Obama. Shortly after getting "my rear end handed to me," as he later put it, he ran successfully for the United States Senate. This time with no sitting Democrat to displace, with abundant planning and with a more experienced campaign staff, including

David Axelrod, a Daley consultant who was the senior political adviser on Obama's campaign for the Democratic presidential nomination.

"Certain Democrats in Chicago say it's the best thing that ever happened to him, not winning that race. He couldn't have been positioned to run for the U.S. Senate from that district," Adelstein said. "In that district, you get pigeonholed pretty quickly as an African-American congressman, not as a more transcendent congressman."

Rush's district, the state's most Democratic, was sixty-five percent black. And in 1999, it included not only Hyde Park, home of the University of Chicago, but several relatively affluent Irish-American neighborhoods.

There were plenty of college-educated, white, "latte liberals" with whom Obama polls well. But he was barely known outside his state Senate district, in the eastern part of Rush's district. To win, he would have to expand his support among blacks, including the older, church-going, Rush loyalists who vote disproportionately in primaries.

"Taking on Bobby Rush among black voters is like running into a buzz saw," said Ron Lester, a pollster who worked for Obama. "This guy was incredibly popular. Not only that, his support ran deep – to the extent that a lot of people who liked Barack still wouldn't support him because they were committed to Bobby. He had built up this reserve of goodwill over twenty-five years in that community."

Rush, who was a Roosevelt University graduate, had grown up in Chicago, enlisted in the Army, joined the Student Nonviolent Coordinating Committee and helped found the Illinois Black Panther Party in 1968. He coordinated a medical clinic that pioneered mass screening for sickle cell anemia, which disproportionately affects blacks. As an alderman in 1992, he had ousted a black political legend – Representative Charles A. Hayes, a former stockyard worker with Dempsey Travis and a veteran of the civil-rights and labor movements, who was caught up in a scandal that year involving the House bank.

Obama, fifteen years younger than Rush, arrived in Chicago in his twenties after growing up in Hawaii and Indonesia. He worked as a community organizer on the Southside for three years, and then returned to the city after graduating from Harvard Law School. He ran a voter registration drive, joined a law firm, taught constitutional law at the University of Chicago and was elected to the state Senate from Hyde Park in 1996.

But he was frustrated at the Statehouse. He had distinguished himself as an ethics reformer there, but it was difficult for Democrats to get much done in a period of virtual Republican lockdown. "He was looking for opportunities to run for offices," said Dan Shomon, who was then a Senate aid.

In February 1999, Rush lost the mayoral primary to Mr. Richard M. Daley, getting just twenty-eight percent of the vote. Toni Preckwinkle, a city alderman, encouraged Obama to challenge Rush.

Shomon said he and Obama did an amateur poll to gauge his chances. They designed questions, recruited volunteers to telephone 300 people, and concluded that Rush was vulnerable. Shomon, who became Obama's campaign manager, said, "Obama will tell you that this poll was not the best poll in the world."

Asked why, he said, "Because the results didn't turn out to be correct."

State senator Terry Link, a friend of Obama, said he advised him not to run. "He tried to justify it: He didn't feel Bobby was representing the area, he thought he could do a better job," Link recalled, "I think he misread it. He didn't analyze the strength of the congressman in that area, the will of the people."

Obama, in a brief telephone interview, said, "In retrospect, there was very little chance of me winning that race. That was a good lesson – that you should never be too impressed with your own ideas if your name recognition in a Congressional district is only eight or whatever it was."

He entered the race in late September, six months before the primary. He told voters that Rush represented 'a politics that is rooted in the past, a reactive politics that isn't good at coming up with concrete solutions." He promised new leadership, reaching beyond the black community and leading coalitions to take on contemporary problems, cut crime, expand health care coverage, promote economic development and expand educational opportunities.

But several weeks later, Lester's polling put Rush's approval rating at seventy percent and Obama's at eight percent. Forty-seven percent of the people polled favored Rush, ten percent favored Obama and five percent favored a third candidate, State Senator Donne E. Trotter, who is also black. Almost all of Obama's support initially came from whites, Lester said.

"Bobby Rush had not been the most active member of Congress from Illinois, but there was no issue that made him particularly vulnerable," Mikva said. "He hadn't robbed a bank or beat his grandmother or things like that. In that respect, I was concerned."

"Also," Mikva said, "I had seen reform candidates running against incumbents in African-American areas. It's hard. Reform is not the most compelling issue to people who don't have a job."

Then in mid–October, Rush's twenty-nine year old son, Huey Rich, was shot on his way home from a grocery store. He hung between life and death for four days. Rush benefited from an outpouring of sympathy; the wake was studded with politicians and there were renewed calls for gun control, one of Rush's causes.

"That incident seemed to wash away any bad feelings that voters had or might have had about Bobby Rush," said Chris Sautter, whose communications firm worked on the Obama campaign.

Later, Gov. George Ryan called the Legislature into special session to try to re-enact a package of gun-safety bills that the Illinois Supreme Court had overturned. Obama was voting consistently in favor of it. But the session dragged on toward Christmas and an annual trip to Hawaii to visit his grandmother, who had helped rear him.

He had planned to return after the holiday when the session was to resume, Shomon said. But a crucial vote came up earlier than expected. With Obama and others absent, it failed by five votes. Obama, in particular, came under fire. In his defense, he said he had not flown back in time because his eighteen month old daughter was sick. But he was hammered by editorial writers, the governor and Rush.

"We were thrown under the bus," Shomon said. "It was a terrible day of news coverage, since, a) we got blasted for not being there and, b) the perception was that Obama doesn't care about gun safety."

In his book *The Audacity of Hope*, Obama wrote, "Less than halfway into the campaign, I knew in my bones that I was going to lose. Each morning, from that point forward, I awoke with a vague sense of dread, realizing that I would have to spend the day smiling and shaking hands and pretending that everything was going according to plan."

Billboards in the district read: "I'm sticking with Bobby." A few black elected officials endorsed Obama but most fell in line behind the incumbent. Ministers closed ranks. The Rev. Michael Pfleger, pastor of the St. Sabina Catholic Church, said other ministers and congregation members called to complain when he endorsed Mr. Obama.

Obama's Ivy League education and his white liberal – establishment connections also became an issue. Rush told *The Chicago Reader*, "He went to Harvard and became an educated fool. We're not impressed with these folks with these Eastern elite degrees."

Rush and his supporters faulted him for having missed experiences that more directly defined the previous generation of black people. "Barack is a person who read about the civil – rights protests and thinks he knows all about it," Rush told *The Reader.*

Obama was seen as an intellectual, "not from us, not from the 'hood," said Jerry Morrison, a consultant on the Rush campaign. Asked recently about that line of attack, Rush minimized it as "chest beating."

The implication was not exactly that Obama was "not black enough," as some blacks have suggested more recently: his credentials were suspect. "It was much more a function of class, not race," Adelstein said, "Nobody said he's not black enough. They said he's a professor, Harvard elite who lives in Hyde Park."

Brian Jackson/Sun Times

Bobby L. Rush, left, Barack Obama and Donne E. Trotter, at a radio show in 2000.

Not everything went badly. Obama proved unusually good at raising money. He raised more than $500,000 – less than Rush but impressive for a newcomer – tapping connections at the University of Chicago, Harvard Law School, law firms where he had worked, and a network of successful, black, Chicago-based entrepreneurs, such as John H. Johnson, Dempsey J. Travis and Al Johnson, who have played an important role in subsequent campaigns.

He was also catching on among whites in the district thanks to Thomas J. Dart, then a popular state representative who is now Cook County Sheriff.

But President Clinton's endorsement of Rush, an early supporter of Clinton, dealt a final blow. Clinton – after a personal request from Rush – overrode his own policy of not endorsing candidates in primaries.

Rush won the primary with just above sixty-one percent of the vote; Obama had just over thirty percent. Obama was favored by whites but lost among blacks, Lester said. Looking back, some say the magnitude of the loss reflected Obama's failure to connect with black, working class voters. Mikva said, "It indicated that he had not made his mark in the African American community and didn't particularly have a style that resonated there."

He and others say Obama learned from that experience. Mikva recalls telling him about advice once given to John F. Kennedy by Cardinal Richard Cushing: "The cardinal said to him, 'Jack, you have to learn to speak more Irish and less Harvard.' I think I recounted that anecdote to Barack. Clearly, he learned how to speak more Chicago and less Harvard in subsequent campaigning."

Shomon said, "There was a gradual progression of Barack Obama from thoughtful, earnest policy work/civil rights lawyer constitutional law expert to Barack Obama the politician, the inspirer, the speaker." Denny Jacobs, a friend of Obama and a former state senator, agreed, "He stumbled on the fact that instead of running on all the issues, quote unquote, that hope is the real key," he said. "Not only the black community, but less privileged people are looking for that hope. You don't have to talk about health care, you have to talk about 'the promise' of health care. Hope is a pretty inclusive word. I think he is very good at selling that."

In March 2004, Obama won the Democratic primary for the United States Senate with nearly fifty-three percent of the vote, racking up huge totals in wards he had lost to Mr. Rush in 2000. Rush, still stung by Obama's challenge to him, endorsed a white candidate in the race, Blair Hull, a former securities trader. Obama won the general election with the biggest margin ever in an Illinois Senate race.

Today, Rush, a practicing Baptist minister in his eighth term in Congress who is backing Obama's presidential candidacy, still seems to be ruminating about the Obama phenomenon with grievance and wonder. Obama's ambition has found its audience, he said. In a Congressional race, your neighbors "hold you to a different standard."

Brendan Smialowski for The New York Times

Barack Obama's biggest political miscalculation is considered to be his 2000 bid against Representative Bobby L. Rush, who is still in office.

"For what he's doing now, he didn't need to march against police brutality," Rush said, invoking his own record. "He didn't need to demonstrate against poor meat in substandard grocery stores. He didn't need that kind of stuff because obviously his audience was at a different level."

Rush has an explanation for Obama's emergence after the dark days of 2000, as a political star four years later. He vanquished a field of multimillionaires, some more experienced and better known, and benefited from fortuitous domestic scandals that sidelined two opponents and left him facing a Republican widely seen as unable to win.

"I would characterize the Senate race as being a race where Obama was, let's say blessed and highly favored," Rush said, chuckling. "That's not routine. There's something else going on."

What was he suggesting?

"I think that Obama, his election to the Senate, was divinely ordered," Rush said, all other explanations failing. "I'm a preacher and a pastor; I know that that was God's plan. Obama has certain qualities that – I think he is being used for some purpose. I really believe that."

In September, an article in a Chicago daily newspaper regarding the Illinois Congressional primary, said that Barack Obama lost in 2000, and misstated the percentage of votes that he and his opponent, Representative Bobby L. Rush, each received. Obama had just above thirty percent, not "less than thirty percent," and Representative Rush had barely over sixty-one percent, not sixty-two percent. The article also misstated the percentage of the vote Obama received in the 2004 Democratic primary for the United State Senate. It was nearly fifty-three percent, not "nearly sixty-seven percent."

CHAPTER 9 – HILLARY CLINTON

Hillary Diane Rodham Clinton is the junior United States Senator from New York, and was a candidate for the Democratic nomination in the 2008 presidential election.

Hillary Diane Rodham was born on October 26, 1947, at Edgewater Hospital in Chicago, Illinois to Hugh Ellsworth Rodham and Dorothy Emma Howell Rodham. Her father was the son of Welsh and English immigrants and operated a small but successful business in the textile industry. Her mother was of English, Scottish, French Canadian, Welsh, and possibly Native American descent, and was a homemaker. Hillary has two younger brothers, Hugh and Tony. She was raised in a United Methodist family, first in Chicago, and then, from the age of three, in suburban Park Ridge, Illinois.

As a child, Hillary Rodham was involved in many activities at church and at her public school in Park Ridge. She participated in tennis and other sports and earned awards as a Brownie and Girl Scout. She attended Maine East High School, where she participated in student council, the debating team and the National Honor Society. For her senior year she was redistricted to Maine South High School, where she was a National Merit Finalist and graduated in 1965. Her parents encouraged her to pursue the career of her choice.

Raised in a politically conservative household, at age thirteen she helped canvass South Side Chicago following the very close 1960 U.S. presidential election, finding evidence of vote fraud against Republican candidate Richard Nixon, and volunteered for Republican candidate Barry Goldwater in the U.S. presidential election of 1964. Her early political development was shaped most strongly by her energizing high school history teacher, like her father a fervent anti-communist, and by her Methodist youth minister, like her mother concerned with issues of social justice. With the minister she saw and met civil rights leader Martin Luther King, Jr. in Chicago in 1962. In response to Hillary Clinton's support of conservative causes in her youth, the question arose regarding how she later became a Democrat. Her mother's response about her own political leanings was simply, "I was a Democrat."

In 1965, Rodham enrolled in Wellesley College, where she majored in political science. Rodham then entered Yale Law School, where she served on the Board of Editors of the *Yale Review of Law* and Social Action. During her second year, she worked at the Yale Child Study Center, learning about new research on early childhood brain development and working as a research assistant on the seminal work, *Beyond the Best Interests of the Child* (1973).

In the late spring of 1971, she began dating Bill Clinton, who was also a law student at Yale. That summer, she interned on child custody cases at the Oakland, California, law firm of Treuhaft, Walker and Burnstein, which was well-known for its support of constitutional rights, civil liberties, and radical causes; two of its four partners were current or former communist party members. Clinton canceled his summer plans to live with her in an apartment in Berkeley, California, later writing, "I told her I'd have the rest of my life for my work and my ambition, but I loved her and I wanted to see if it could work out for us." The romance did develop, and the couple continued living together in New Haven when they returned to law school. The following summer, Rodham and Clinton campaigned in Texas for unsuccessful 1972 Democratic presidential candidate George McGovern. She received a Juris Doctor degree from Yale in 1973, having spent an extra year there in order to be with Clinton. Clinton first proposed marriage to her following graduation, but she declined at the time. She began a year of post-graduate study on children and medicine at the Yale Child Study Center. Her first scholarly paper, "Children Under the Law," was published in the *Harvard Educational Review* in late 1973 and became frequently cited in the field.

Meanwhile, Clinton had repeatedly asked her to marry him, and she had continued to defer. However, helped by her having passed the Arkansas bar exam but having failed the District of Columbia bar exam, Rodham came to a key decision. As she later wrote, "I chose to follow my heart instead of my head." She thus followed Bill Clinton to Arkansas, rather than staying in Washington where career prospects were best. Clinton was at the time teaching law and running for a seat in the U.S. House of Representatives in his home state. In August 1974, she moved to Fayetteville, Arkansas, and became one of two female faculty members at the University of Arkansas, Fayetteville School of Law, where Bill Clinton also taught. Even then, she still harbored doubts about marriage, concerned that her separate identity would be lost and her accomplishments would be viewed in the light of someone else's accomplishments.

The couple bought a house in Fayetteville in the summer of 1975, and she finally agreed to marry him. Hillary Rodham and Bill Clinton were married on October 11, 1975, in a Methodist ceremony in their living room. She kept her name as Hillary Rodham, later writing that she had done so to keep their professional lives separate and avoid seeming conflicts of interest, although it upset both their mothers. Bill Clinton had lost the Congressional race in 1974, but in November, 1976, he was elected Attorney General of Arkansas. This required the couple to move to the state capital of Little Rock. Rodham joined the venerable Rose Law Firm, a bastion of Arkansan political and economic influence, in February 1977, specializing in patent infringement and intellectual property law, while also working pro bono in child advocacy; she rarely performed litigation work in court.

Following the November, 1978 election of her husband as Governor of Arkansas, Rodham became First Lady of Arkansas in January, 1979, her title for a total of twelve years (1979–1981, 1983–1992). Clinton appointed her chair of the Rural Health Advisory Committee the same year, where she successfully obtained federal funds to expand medical facilities in Arkansas' poorest areas without affecting doctors' fees.

On February 27, 1980, Rodham gave birth to a daughter, Chelsea, her only child. In November, 1980, Bill Clinton was defeated in his bid for re-election.

Bill Clinton returned to the Governor's office two years later by winning the election of 1982. During her husband's campaign, Rodham began to use the name Hillary Clinton, or sometimes "Mrs. Bill Clinton," in order to have greater appeal to Arkansas voters. She also took a leave of absence from Rose Law in order to campaign for him full-time. As First Lady of Arkansas, Hillary Clinton chaired the Arkansas Educational Standards Committee from 1982 to 1992, where she sought to bring about reform in the state's court-sanctioned public education system. In one of the most important initiatives of the entire Clinton governorship, she fought a prolonged but ultimately successful battle against the Arkansas Education Association to put mandatory teacher testing as well as state standards for curriculum and classroom size in place. She introduced Arkansas' Home Instruction Program for Preschool Youth in 1985, a program that helps parents work with their children in preschool preparedness and literacy. She was named Arkansas Woman of the Year in 1983 and Arkansas Mother of the Year in 1984.

Clinton served on the boards of the Arkansas Children's Hospital Legal Services (1988–1992) and the Children's Defense Fund (as chair, 1986–1992). In addition to her positions with non-profit organizations, she also held positions on the corporate board of directors of TCBY (1985–1992), Wal-Mart Stores (1986–1992) and Lafarge (1990–1992). TCBY and Wal-Mart were Arkansas-based companies that were also clients of Rose Law. Clinton was the first female member on Wal-Mart's board, added when Chairman Sam Walton was pressured to name one. Once there, she pushed successfully for the chain to adopt more environmentally-friendly practices, pushed largely unsuccessfully for more women to be added to the company's management, and was silent about the company's famously anti-labor union practices.

After her husband became a candidate for the Democratic presidential nomination of 1992, Hillary Clinton received popular national attention for the first time. Before the New Hampshire primary, tabloid publications printed claims that Bill Clinton had had an extramarital affair with Gennifer Flowers, an Arkansas lounge singer. In response, the Clintons appeared together on 60 Minutes, during which Bill Clinton denied the affair but acknowledged he had caused "pain" in their marriage. (Years later, he would admit that the Flowers affair had happened, but to lesser extent than she claimed). Hillary Clinton made culturally dismissive remarks about Tammy Wynette and baking cookies and having teas during the campaign that were ill-considered by her own admission. Bill Clinton said that electing him would get "two for the price of one," referring to the prominent role his wife would assume.

When Bill Clinton took office as president in January 1993, Hillary Rodham Clinton became the First Lady of the United States, and announced that she would be using that form of her name. She was the initial first lady to hold a post-graduate degree and to have her own professional career up to the time of entering the White House. She was also the initial first lady to take up an office in the West Wing of the White House - first ladies usually staying in the East Wing. She is regarded as the most openly empowered presidential wife in American history, save for Eleanor Roosevelt.

Some critics called it inappropriate for the First Lady to play a central role in matters of public policy. Supporters pointed out that Clinton's role in policy was no different from that of other White House advisors and that voters were well aware that she would play an active role in her husband's Presidency. Bill Clinton's campaign as "co-presidents," or sometimes "Billary." The pressures of conflicting ideas about the role of a First Lady were enough to send Clinton into "imaginary discussions" with the also-politically-active Eleanor Roosevelt. From the time she came to Washington, she also found refuge in a prayer group of The Fellowship that featured many wives of conservative Washington figures. Triggered in part by the death of her father in April, 1993, she publicly sought to find a synthesis of Methodist teachings, liberal religious political philosophy, and Tikkun editor Michael Lerner's "politics of meaning" to overcome what she saw as America's "sleeping sickness of the soul."

The Clinton family takes an Inauguration Day walk down Pennsylvania Avenue to start Bill Clinton's second term in office. January 20, 1997.

That would lead to a willingness "to remold society by redefining what it means to be a human being in the twentieth century, moving into a new millennium." Other segments of the public focused on her appearance, which had evolved over time from inattention to fashion during her days in Arkansas, to a popular site in the early days of the World Wide Web devoted to showing her many different, and much analyzed, hairstyles as First Lady, to an appearance on the cover of Vogue magazine in 1998.

In 1993, the president appointed his wife to head and be the chairwoman of the Task Force on National Health Care Reform, hoping to replicate the success she had in leading the effort for Arkansas education reform. The recommendation of the task force became known as the Clinton Health Care Plan, a complex proposal that would mandate employers to provide health coverage to their employees through individual health maintenance organizations. The plan was quickly derided as "Hillarycare" by its opponents; some protesters against it became vitriolic, and during a July, 1994 bus tour to rally support for the plan, she was forced to wear a bulletproof vest at times. The plan did not receive enough support for a floor vote in either the House or the Senate, although both chambers were controlled by Democrats, and proposal was abandoned in September of 1994. Clinton later acknowledged in her book, *Living History*, that her political inexperience partly contributed to the defeat, but mentioned that many other factors were also responsible. The First Lady's approval ratings, which had generally been in the high-50s percent range during her first year, fell to forty-four percent in April, 1994 and thirty-five percent by September, 1994. Republicans made the Clinton health care plan a major campaign issue of the 1994 midterm elections, which saw a net Republican gain of fifty-three seats in the House election and seven in the Senate election, winning control of both; many analysts and pollsters found the plan to be a major factor in the Democrats' defeat, especially among independent voters. Opponents of universal health care would continue to use "Hillarycare" as a pejorative label for similar plans by others.

The Whitewater controversy was the focus of media attention from the publication of a *New York Times* report during the 1992 presidential campaign, and throughout her time as First Lady. The Clintons had lost their late-1970's investment in the Whitewater Development Corporation; at the same time, their partners in that investment, Jim and Susan McDougal, operated Madison Guaranty, a savings and loan institution that retained the legal services of Rose Law Firm and may have been improperly subsidizing Whitewater losses. Madison Guaranty later failed, and Clinton's work at Rose was scrutinized for a possible conflict of interest in representing the bank before state regulators that her husband had appointed; she claimed she had done minimal work for the bank. Independent counsels Robert Fiske and Kenneth Starr subpoenaed Clinton's legal billing records; she claimed to be unable to produce these records. The records were found in the First Lady's White House book room after a two-year search, and delivered to investigators in early 1996. The delayed appearance of the records sparked intense interest and another investigation about how they surfaced and where they had been. Clinton attributed the problem to disorganization that resulted from their move from the Arkansas Governor's Mansion and the effects of a White House renovation. After the discovery of the records, on January 26, 1996, Clinton made history by becoming the first First Lady to be subpoenaed to testify before a Federal grand jury. After several Independent Counsels investigated, a final report was issued in 2000 which stated that there was insufficient evidence that either Clinton had engaged in criminal wrongdoing.

Other investigations took place during Hillary Clinton's time as First Lady. Scrutiny of the May, 1993 firings of the White House Travel Office employees, an affair that became known as "Travelgate," began with charges that the White House had used alleged financial improprieties in the Travel Office operation as an excuse to replace the office staff and give the White House travel business to Arkansas friends of theirs. Over the years the investigation focused more on whether Hillary Clinton had orchestrated the firings and whether the statements she made to investigating authorities regarding her role in the firings were true. The 2000 final Independent Counsel report found that there was substantial evidence that she was involved in the firings and that she had made "factually false" statements, but that there was insufficient evidence to prosecute her. Following deputy White House counsel Vince Foster's July, 1993 suicide, allegations were made that Hillary Clinton had ordered the removal of potentially damaging files (related to Whitewater or other matters) from Foster's office on the night of his death. Independent Counsel Kenneth Starr investigated this, and by 1999, Starr was reported to be holding the investigation open, despite his staff having told him there was no case to be made. When Starr's successor, Robert Ray, issued his final Whitewater reports in 2000, no claims were made against Hillary Clinton regarding this. In March, 1994, newspaper reports revealed her spectacular profits from cattle futures trading in 1978–1979; allegations were made of conflict of interest and disguised bribery, and several individuals analyzed her trading records, but no official investigation was made and she was never charged with any wrongdoing.

An outgrowth of the Travelgate investigation was the June 1996 discovery of improper White House access to hundreds of FBI background reports on former Republican White House employees, an affair that some called "Filegate." Accusations were made that Hillary Clinton had requested these files and that she had recommended hiring an unqualified individual to head the White House Security Office. The 2000 final Independent Counsel report found no substantial or credible evidence that Hillary Clinton had any role or showed any misconduct in the matter.

In 1998, the Clintons' relationship became the subject of much speculation and gossip when it was revealed that the President had had an extramarital affair with White House intern Monica Lewinsky. When the allegations against her husband were first made public, Hillary Clinton stated that they were the result of a "vast right-wing conspiracy," characterizing the Lewinsky charges as the latest in a long, organized, collaborative series of charges by Clinton political enemies, rather than any wrongdoing by her husband. She later said that she had been misled by her husband's initial claims that no affair had taken place. After the evidence of President Clinton's encounters with Lewinsky became incontrovertible and he admitted to her his unfaithful behavior, she issued a public statement reaffirming her commitment to their marriage, but privately was reported to be furious at him and was unsure if she wanted to stay in the marriage.

There was a mix of public reactions to Hillary Clinton after this. Some women admired her strength and poise in private matters made public. Some sympathized with her as a victim of her husband's insensitive behavior. Others criticized her as being an enabler to her husband's indiscretions by not obtaining a divorce, while still others accused her of cynically staying in a failed marriage as a way of keeping or even fostering her own political influence. Overall, her public approval ratings in the wake of the revelations shot upward to seventy-one percent, the highest they had ever been. In her 2003 memoir, she would attribute her decision to stay married to love, "No one understands me better and no one can make me laugh the way Bill does. Even after all these years, he is still the most interesting, energizing and fully alive person I have ever met."

The long-serving United States Senator from New York, Daniel Patrick Moynihan, announced his retirement in November 1998. Several prominent Democratic figures, including Representative Charles Rangel of New York, urged Clinton to run for Moynihan's open seat in the United States Senate election of 2000. When she decided to run, Clinton and her husband purchased a home in Chappaqua, New York, north of New York City in September 1999. She became the first First Lady of the United States to be a candidate for elected office. At first, Clinton was expected to face Rudy Giuliani, the Mayor of New York City, as her Republican opponent in the election. However, Giuliani withdrew from the race after being diagnosed with prostate cancer, and Clinton instead faced Rick Lazio, a Republican member of the United States House of Representatives representing New York's 2nd congressional district. Throughout the campaign and during debates, Clinton was accused of carpet bagging by her opponents, as she had never resided in New York nor participated in the state's politics prior to this race. However, there was precedent for her action: New York had elected Robert F. Kennedy senator in 1964 despite similar accusations. Clinton began her campaign by visiting every county in the state, in a "listening tour" of small-group settings. During the campaign, she devoted considerable time in traditionally Republican Upstate New York regions. Clinton vowed to improve the economic situation in those areas, promising to deliver 200,000 jobs to the state over her term. Her plan included specific tax credits to reward job creation and encourage business investment, especially in the high-tech sector. She called for personal tax cuts for college tuition and long-term care.

The contest drew national attention and both candidates were well-funded. Clinton secured a broad base of support, including endorsements from conservation groups and organized labor, but not the New York City police and firefighters' unions. By the date of the election, the campaigns of Clinton and Lazio, along with Giuliani's initial effort, had spent a combined $78 million. Clinton won the election on November 7, 2000, with fifty-five percent of the vote to Lazio's forty-three percent. She was sworn in as United States Senator on January 3, 2001.

Upon entering the United States Senate, Clinton maintained a low public profile while building relationships with senators from both parties, to avoid the polarizing celebrity she experienced as First Lady. Clinton also forged alliances with religiously-inclined senators by becoming a regular participant in the Senate Prayer Breakfast.

Clinton has served on five Senate committees: Committee on Budget (2001–2002), Committee on Armed Services (since 2003), Committee on Environment and Public Works (since 2001), Committee on Health, Education, Labor and Pensions (since 2001) and Special Committee on Aging. She is also a Commissioner of the Commission on Security and Cooperation in Europe (since 2001).

As a member of the Senate Committee on Armed Services, Clinton strongly supported military action in Afghanistan, saying it was a chance to combat terrorism while improving the lives of Afghan women who suffered under the Taliban government. Clinton voted in favor of the October, 2002 Iraq War Resolution, which authorized United States President George W. Bush to use military force against Iraq, should such action be required to enforce a United Nations Security Council Resolution after pursuing with diplomatic efforts.

However, Clinton voted against the Levin Amendment to the Resolution, which would have required the President to conduct vigorous diplomacy at the U.N., and would have also required a separate Congressional authorization to unilaterally invade Iraq. She did vote for the Byrd Amendment to the Resolution, which would have limited the Congressional authorization to one year increments, but the only mechanism necessary for the President to renew his mandate without any Congressional oversight was to claim that the Iraq War was vital to national security each year the authorization required renewal.

After the Iraq War began, Clinton made trips to both Iraq and Afghanistan to visit American troops stationed there, such as the 10th Mountain Division based in Fort Drum, New York. On a visit to Iraq in February 2005, Clinton noted that the insurgency had failed to disrupt the democratic elections held earlier, and that parts of the country were functioning well. Noting that war deployments are draining regular and reserve forces, she co-introduced legisla

Hillary Rodham Clinton being sworn in as a U.S. Senator by V.P. Al Gore in the Old Senate Chamber, as President Clinton and daughter Chelsea look on. January 3, 2001.

tion to increase the size of the regular United States Army by 80,000 soldiers to ease the strain.

In late 2005, Clinton said that while immediate withdrawal from Iraq would be a mistake, Bush's pledge to stay "until the job is done" is also misguided, as it gives Iraqis "an open-ended invitation not to take care of themselves." She criticized the administration for making poor decisions in the war, but added that it was more important to solve the problems in Iraq. This centrist and somewhat vague stance caused frustration among those in the Democratic Party who favor immediate withdrawal. Clinton supported retaining and improving health benefits for veterans, and lobbied against the closure of several military bases.

Senator Clinton voted against the tax cuts introduced by President Bush, including the Economic Growth and Tax Relief Reconciliation Act of 2001 and the Jobs and Growth Tax Relief Reconciliation Act of 2003, saying it was fiscally irresponsible to reopen the budget deficit.

In November, 2004, Clinton announced that she would seek a second term in the United States Senate. She won the election on November 7, 2006, with sixty-seven percent of the vote to Spencer's thirty-one percent, carrying all but four of New York's sixty-two counties. Clinton spent $36 million towards her re-election, more than any other candidate for Senate in the 2006 elections. She was criticized by some Democrats for spending too much in a one-sided contest, while some supporters were concerned she did not leave more funds for a potential presidential bid in 2008. In the following months she transferred $10 million of her Senate funds towards her now-official presidential campaign.

Clinton has enjoyed high approval ratings for her job as senator within New York, reaching an all-time high of seventy-two to seventy-four percent approving (including half of Republicans) over twenty-three to twenty-four percent disapproving in December, 2006, before her presidential campaign became active. By August, 2007, after a half year of campaigning, it was still sixty-four percent over thirty-four percent.

Clinton had been mentioned as a potential candidate for United States President since at least October, 2002. She has been ranked among the world's most powerful people by *Forbes Magazine* and *Time Magazine's* Time 100. On January 20, 2007, Clinton announced on her Web site the formation of a presidential exploratory committee, with the intention to become a candidate for president in the United States presidential election of 2008. In her announcement, she stated, "I'm in. And I'm in to win." No woman has ever been nominated by a major party for President of the United States.

Clinton led the field of candidates competing for the Democratic nomination in opinion polls for the election throughout the first half of 2007. Most polls placed Senator Barack Obama of Illinois and former Senator John Edwards of North Carolina as Clinton's closest competitors in the early caucus and primary election states. Clinton set records for early fundraising, which Obama then topped in the following months before Clinton later regained the money lead, but Clinton generally maintained her lead in the polls.

In April, 2007, the Clintons liquidated a blind trust that had been established when he became president in 1993, in order to avoid the possibility of ethical conflicts or political embarrassments in the trust as Hillary Clinton undertook her presidential race. Later disclosure

Hillary Clinton campaigning, 2007

statements revealed that the couple's worth was now upwards of $50 million. In late August, 2007, a major contributor to, and "bundler" for, Clinton's campaign, called a "HillRaiser," Norman Hsu, was revealed to be a fifteen-years-long fugitive in an investment fraud case. He was also suspected of having broken campaign finance law regarding his bundling collections. The Clinton campaign first said it would donate to charity the $23,000 that Hsu personally contributed to her, then said it would refund to 260 donors the full $850,000 in bundled donations raised by Hsu. Hsu was subsequently indicted on new investment fraud charges.

By September, 2007, opinion polling in the first six states holding Democratic primaries or caucuses showed that Clinton was leading in all of them, with the races being closest in Iowa and South Carolina. By October, 2007, national polls had Clinton far ahead of any Democratic competitor. At the end of October, Clinton suffered what writers for *The Washington Post*, ABC News, *The Politico*, and other outlets characterized as a rare poor debate performance as she was attacked by Obama, Edwards, and her other opponents. Subsequently, the race tightened considerably, especially in the early caucus and primary states of Iowa, New Hampshire, and South Carolina, and by December Clinton was losing her lead in some polls.

On what is known as “Super Tuesday,” February 5, 2008, Clinton won the delegate-rich states when twenty-two contests were held simultaneously. Clinton took New York, California, Massachusetts, and New Jersey. But the next day, on February 6, her campaign revealed she had been out-fundraised by her rival and that she was out of campaign cash. She lent her campaign $5 million of her own money. Clinton did so again on May 17, 2008, as more superdelegates started turning to Obama, giving herself $6.4 million. It wasn’t enough. On June 3, 2008, Clinton won big in South Dakota but Obama won Montana. Superdelegates start flooding to Obama and he crosses the magic delegate number of 2,118. Five days later, on June 8, 2008, Clinton exited the campaign and endorsed Barack Obama for president. She encouraged her supporters to embrace unity in the Democratic Party by also supporting Obama, though many were reluctant to do so.

CHAPTER 10 – BARACK OBAMA IN POLITICS

It has been the rich and varied experiences of Barack Obama's life - growing up in different places with people who had differing ideas - that have animated his political journey. Amid the partisanship and bickering of today's public debate, he still believes in the ability to unite people around a politics of purpose - a politics that puts solving the challenges of everyday Americans ahead of partisan calculation and political gain.

Barack Obama's advocacy throughout his college years and after led him to run for the Illinois State Senate as a Democrat for the 1996 election. He was elected from the south side neighborhood of Hyde Park in Chicago. During his time in the Senate, he worked with both Democrats and Republicans in drafting legislation on ethics, expanded health care services and early childhood education programs for the poor. He also created a state earned-income tax credit for the working poor, which in three years provided over $100 million in tax cuts to families across the state. After a number of death row inmates were found innocent, Obama worked with officials of law enforcement to require that all confessions and interrogations of capital cases be videotaped. Barack also served as chairman of the Public Health and Welfare Committee. From 1993, throughout his Senate career, Obama also taught constitutional law part-time at the University of Chicago Law School, as a Lecturer from 1992 to 1996, and as a Senior Lecturer from 1996 to 2004. After being defeated in the primary by Jesse Jackson, Jr., Alice Palmer requested that Obama drop out of the race and let her run for the seat. Obama declined and Palmer decided to run against him. Prior to the primary, Obama challenged the validity of ballot petition signatures for his opponents, resulting in their exclusion from the ballot and allowing him to run unopposed in the primary. Obama won the heavily Democratic thirteenth district by a large margin.

He received advice from some powerful mentors during his state Senate career. Early in his first term, the just-retired U.S. Senator Paul Simon called a longtime Obama mentor, judge and former congressman Abner Mikva. Simon suggested that Mikva recommend Obama to Emil Jones, Jr., the powerful Democratic leader of the state Senate. "'Say, our friend Barack Obama has a chance to push this campaign finance bill through,'" Simon said in a telephone conversation, as recounted by Mikva in a 2008 interview. "'Why don't you call your friend Emil Jones and tell him how good he is?'" With Jones' support, Obama successfully passed a sweeping law that banned most gifts from lobbyists and personal use of campaign funds by state legislators. It was one of his most prominent bills in the state Senate.

As a state legislator, Obama gained bipartisan support for legislation reforming ethics and health care laws. He sponsored a law enhancing tax credits for low-income workers, negotiated welfare reform and promoted increased subsidies for childcare.

In 2000, Obama made a Democratic primary run for the U.S. House of Representatives seat held by four-term incumbent candidate Bobby Rush. Rush had been badly defeated in the February 1999 Chicago Mayoral election by Richard M. Daley and was thought to be vulnerable. In 1999, Obama asked his friend and mentor, Newton Minow to help him raise funds for the race, and Minow complied, but the fund-raising effort bombed. During the campaign, Rush charged that Obama was not sufficiently rooted in Chicago's black neighborhoods to represent constituents' concerns, and also benefitted from an outpouring of sympathy when his son was shot to death shortly before the election. Obama said Rush was a part of "a politics that is rooted in the past" and said he himself could build bridges with whites to get things done. But while Obama did well in his own Hyde Park base, he didn't get enough support from the surrounding black neighborhoods. Starting with just ten percent name recognition, Obama went on to get only thirty-one percent of the votes, losing by a more than two-to-one margin despite winning among white voters. The Rev. Michael Pfleger, a controversial but influential Catholic priest, was one of the few South Side clergymen to support Obama in the race. After Obama lost, he sponsored a $100,000 earmark to help finance a youth center associated with Pfleger's church. The program was one of many worthy efforts Pfleger's church was organizing, according to Obama's 2008 presidential campaign organization.

After losing the primary for U.S. Congress to Bobby Rush, Obama worked to repair relations with black politicians and clergy members, telling them he bore no grudges against the victor. He also became more responsive to requests for state funding, getting money for churches and community groups in his district. State Senator Donne E. Trotter, then the top Democrat on the Senate Appropriations Committee, said in 2008 that he knew Obama was responding more to funding requests "because the community groups in his district stopped coming to me."

When Democrats took control of the state Senate in the 2002 elections, Obama became chairman of the Health and Human Services Committee in January 2003. Jones supported Obama's sponsorship of proposed laws important to blacks, like requiring police to tape interrogations. Obama was willing to negotiate compromises to get the law passed, including a large number of exemptions. That helped him develop a reputation as a pragmatist able to work with various sides of an issue. Obama also led the passage of a law to monitor racial profiling by requiring police to record the race of drivers they stopped.

Following the 9/11 attacks, Obama was an early opponent of President George W. Bush's push to war with Iraq. Obama was still a state senator when he spoke against a resolution authorizing the use of force against Iraq during a rally at Chicago's Federal Plaza in October 2002. "I am not opposed to all wars. I'm opposed to dumb wars," he said. "What I am opposed to is the cynical attempt by Richard Perle and Paul Wolfowitz and other armchair, weekend warriors in this Administration to shove their own ideological agendas down our throats, irrespective of the costs in lives lost and in hardships borne. He's a bad guy," Obama said, referring to Iraqi dictator Saddam Hussein. "The world, and the Iraqi people, would be better off without him. But I also know that Saddam poses no imminent and direct threat to the United States, or to his neighbors, that the Iraqi economy is in shambles, that the Iraqi military is a fraction of its former strength, and that in concert with the international community he can be contained until, in the way of all petty dictators, he falls away into the dustbin of history. I know that even a successful war against Iraq will require a U. S. occupation of undetermined length, at undetermined cost, with undetermined consequences," Obama continued.

Brendan Smialowski for The New York Times

Bobby L. Rush, still in office in 2007.

"I know that an invasion of Iraq without a clear rationale and without strong international support will only fan the flames of the Middle East, and encourage the worst, rather than best, impulses of the Arab world, and strengthen the recruitment arm of al-Qaeda."

The war with Iraq began in 2003 and Obama decided to run for the U.S. Senate open seat vacated by Republican Peter Fitzgerald. His opponent in the general election was supposed to be Republican primary winner Jack Ryan, a wealthy former investment banker. However, Ryan withdrew from the race in June 2004, following public disclosure of unsubstantiated sexual allegations by Ryan's ex wife, actress Jeri Ryan. In August 2004, diplomat and former presidential candidate Alan Keyes, who was also an African American, accepted the Republican nomination to replace Ryan. In three televised debates, Obama and Keyes expressed opposing views on stem cell research, abortion, gun control, school vouchers and tax cuts.

During the general election campaign for U.S. Senate, he won the endorsement of the Illinois Fraternal Order of Police, whose president credited Obama for his active engagement with police organizations in enacting death penalty reforms. He was criticized by rival pro-choice candidates in the Democratic primary and by his Republican pro-life opponent in the general election for a series of "present" or "no" votes on late-term abortion and parental notification issues. In the 2004 Democratic primary, he won fifty-two percent of the vote, defeating multimillionaire businessman Blair Hull and Illinois Comptroller Daniel Hynes.

In the November 2004 general election, Obama received seventy percent of the vote to Keyes' twenty-seven percent, the largest electoral victory in Illinois history. Obama became only the third African-American elected to the U.S. Senate since Reconstruction. He resigned from the Illinois Senate in November 2004, following his election to the U.S. Senate.

That summer, he was invited to deliver the keynote speech in support of John Kerry at the 2004 Democratic National Convention in Boston. Obama emphasized the importance of unity, and made veiled jabs at the Bush administration and the diversionary use of wedge issues.

"We worship an awesome God in the blue states, and we don't like federal agents poking around our libraries in the red states," he said. "We coach Little League in the blue states, and yes, we've got some gay friends in the red states. There are patriots who opposed the war in Iraq, and there are patriots who supported the war in Iraq. We are one people, all of us pledging allegiance to the Stars and Stripes, all of us defending the United States of America."

M. Spencer Green/Associated Press

Mr. Obama with his wife and daughter Sasha the night of the primary

John Gress/Reuters

The Obama family celebrating the victory at their election headquarters in Chicago

Chang W. Lee/The New York Times

Obama at the DNC in Boston, 2004

Mr. Obama listening to testimony in an Illinois Senate hearing.

After the convention, Obama returned to his U.S. Senate bid in Illinois. He was sworn into office January 4, 2005, and *Time* magazine named him "one of the world's most influential people," calling him "one of the most admired politicians in America" just four months into his Senate career. Obama partnered with Republican Sen. Richard Lugar of Indiana on a bill that expanded efforts to destroy weapons of mass destruction in Eastern Europe and Russia. Then with Republican Sen. Tom Corburn of Oklahoma, he created a website that tracks all federal spending, allowing every American to go online and see how and where every dime of their tax dollars is spent. Obama was also the first to raise the threat of avian flu on the Senate floor, spoke out for victims of Hurricane Katrina, pushed for alternative energy development and championed improved veterans′ benefits. He also worked with Democrat Russ Feingold of Wisconsin to eliminate gifts of travel on corporate jets by lobbyists to members of Congress. He has focused on tackling the challenges of a globalized, twenty-first century world with fresh thinking and a politics that no longer settles for the lowest common denominator.

As a member of the Veterans' Affairs Committee, Senator Obama has fought to help Illinois veterans get the disability pay they were promised, while working to prepare the VA for the return of the thousands of veterans who will need care after Iraq and Afghanistan. Recognizing the terrorist threat posed by weapons of mass destruction, he traveled to Russia with Republican Dick Lugar to begin a new generation of non-proliferation efforts designed to find and secure deadly weapons around the world. And knowing the threat we face to our economy and

A supporter held up Mr. Obama's second best-selling book at a rally in April, 2008

our security from America's addiction to oil, he's working to bring auto companies, unions, farmers, businesses and politicians of both parties together to promote the greater use of alternative fuels and higher fuel standards in our cars.

In December 2004, Barack signed a contract to write three more books. Obama's second book, the first of the three, is titled *The Audacity of Hope: Thoughts on Reclaiming the American Dream*, and was published in October 2006. The book has remained at or near the top of the New York Times Best Seller list since its publication. It was also the theme of his 2004 keynote address. The second book will be a children's book to be co-written with his wife Michelle and their two daughters, with profits going to charity. The content of the third book has yet to be announced.

In August, 2006, Obama traveled to Kenya, Africa, his father's home country. There, thousands lined the streets to greet him. He also visited South Africa, Chad, and Djibouti.

On October 22, 2006, he told anchorman Tim Russert that he was reconsidering the possibility of running for president after previously going on the record to say he would not run. On December 10, he made his first visit to New Hampshire, riding a wave of publicity in anticipation of a potential presidential bid. He drew sell-out crowds. On January 16, 2007, Obama entered the race for the White House and announced he was forming an exploratory committee. On February 10, 2007, he made headlines when he announced his candidacy for the 2008 Democratic presidential nomination on the steps of the Old State Capital in Springfield, Illinois. This is the same spot where Abraham Lincoln once declared that a house divided against itself cannot stand.

Shortly after announcing his candidacy, Senators Barack Obama and Hillary Rodham Clinton evoked the passions and rivalries of the civil rights era, making deeply personal appeals to voters in the sanctuaries of black churches in Selma, Alabama, on March 4. Afterwards, they joined former President Bill Clinton for a march across a bridge where white police officers beat protestors, most of them black, forty-two years ago. The Clintons and Senator Obama walked with two black congressmen and others down Martin Luther King Jr. Street to commemorate the footsteps of black demonstrators who were met with violence as they tried to march to Montgomery to demand civil rights in 1965.

It was the first side-by-side appearance of Obama and Clinton in the 2008 presidential campaign. Obama and Clinton spoke at services on the same street, three blocks apart, and the lines of worshipers were so long that they nearly intermingled. Both candidates paid homage to the same civil rights leaders, and both concluded the services by locking arms with worshipers and swaying to "We Shall Overcome." At different points, both Clintons said that the Voting Rights Act of 1965 had paved the way for Obama to run for president.

"Today it is giving Senator Obama the chance to run for president," Clinton told worshipers at the First Baptist Church, to enthusiastic applause. "And by its logic and spirit, it is giving the same chance to Gov. Bill Richardson to run as a Hispanic. And, yes, it is giving me that chance."

Obama and Clinton had one overarching theme in their remarks: the honoring of the civil rights movement that had contributed to their own rise in politics and quests for the nomination.

"We're in the presence today of giants whose shoulders we stand on," Obama said at the Brown Chapel A.M.E. Church. "People who battled on behalf not just of African-Americans but on behalf of all Americans, who battled for America's soul, that shed blood, that endured taunts and torment."

In a thirty-five minute address, Obama said it was time for his generation to pick up the work of those who had toiled before. He said it was time for the "Joshua generation" — a biblical reference to the leader who succeeded Moses — to urge family and friends to shake their apathy to engage in politics and action.

"I know if cousin Pookie would vote, if brother Jethro would get off the couch and stop watching Sports-Center and go register some folks and go to the polls, we'd have a different kind of politics," Obama said, the crowd rising to its feet. "Kick off your bedroom slippers, put on your marching shoes!"

Down the street, meanwhile, the congregation warmly welcomed Clinton, who blended personal anecdotes with a fluidly thematic set of remarks, in which she said the civil rights march "is not over yet. Poverty and growing inequality matter. Health care matters. The people of the Gulf Coast matter. Our soldiers matter. Our future matters."

Both candidates, too, turned to stories from their past to show their connection to the civil rights movement. There was controversy over Obama's story of how his Kenyan father and his Kansan mother fell in love because of the tumult of Selma, but he was born in 1961, four years before the confrontation at Selma took place. When asked later, Obama clarified himself, saying: "I meant the whole civil rights movement." He also acknowledged for the first time a revelation by a genealogist that his mother's ancestors in Kentucky owned slaves.

Senator Barack Obama joined Representative John Lewis in singing at church in Selma, Ala. on Sunday.

Senators Barack Obama and Hillary Rodham Clinton and former President Bill Clinton participated in a commemorative march in Selma.

"It turns out that her great-great-great-great-grandfather actually owned slaves," Obama said before another audience, over breakfast, at George C. Wallace Community College. That's no surprise. That's part of our tortured, tangled history."

Clinton recalled going with her church youth minister as a teenager in 1963 to hear the Rev. Martin Luther King Jr. speak in Chicago. However, in her autobiography and elsewhere, Mrs. Clinton has described growing up Republican and being a "Goldwater Girl" in 1964 — in other words, a supporter of the presidential candidacy of Senator Barry M. Goldwater, who opposed the 1964 Civil Rights Act.

Obama, followed by large entourages and curious onlookers, had come to Selma three days before the anniversary of Bloody Sunday, a violent afternoon near the Edmund Pettus Bridge that became a turning point in the American civil rights movement. As they re-enacted the 1965 march, making their way to the Alabama River, the Clintons were at the front of the assembly, while Mr. Obama was often only two people away, separated by John Lewis and Artur Davis, the Democratic congressmen from Georgia and Alabama. They were all linked arm in arm throughout as they slowly moved forward on the two-mile walk.

Civil rights leader Jesse Jackson endorsed Obama in his presidential bid, giving his support to a new generation of black politicians. "He has my vote," the Rev. Jackson told The Associated Press in a telephone interview on March 29, 2007. Many believed that Jackson's endorsement would help Obama to secure black votes. However, during the controversial arrest of six black kids arrested on attempted murder charges in Jena, Louisiana, Jackson ripped Obama for "acting like he's white" by failing to bring attention to the matter on September 19, 2007.

Jackson later said he did not recall the comment and said, "I reaffirm my commitment to vote for Sen. Barack Obama. I think Jena is another defining moment of the issue of race and the criminal justice system. This issue requires direct and bold leadership. I commend Sen. Obama for speaking out and demanding fairness on this defining issue. Any attempt to dilute my support for Sen. Obama will not succeed."

Again in July, 2008, Jackson had to apologize for "crude and hurtful" remarks he made about Obama after an interview with a Fox News correspondent. The remarks came as Jackson was talking to a fellow interviewee, United Health Group executive Dr. Reed V. Tuckson. An open microphone picked up Jackson whispering, "See, Barack's been talking down to black people ... I want to cut his nuts off." Jackson claimed his comment was in relation to Obama's speech in which he called absent black fathers to task, saying, "We need them to realize that what makes you a man is not the ability to have a child – it's the courage to raise one."

On May 3, 2007, the Secret Service began guarding Obama. This was the earliest a presidential candidate had ever been provided protection. While no specific threats had been made to Obama at that time, the request came from a cumulative effect of a heavier campaign schedule and larger crowds. Secret Service protection included surrounding the candidate with well-armed agents and extensive advance work and threat assessments developed by its intelligence division to identify potential risks.

Photo courtesy Matthew Lawrence, Obama Staff Intern, Greenwood, South Carolina
Secret Service outside the Stage during an Obama Visit to Pee Dee, SC

At the end of the second quarter, on June 30, 2007, Obama announced he had raised at least $32.5 million, topping his first quarter effort by nearly $7 million. The amount is believed to be the highest ever raised in a quarter by a Democratic candidate and exceeded what Clinton's campaign predicted she would raise during the same period. More than 154,000 donors contributed to Obama's campaign during the second quarter, up from the 104,000 donors in the first quarter, in which he raised $25.7 million.

Obama proposed a plan on September 18, 2007, to provide at least $80 billion a year in tax cuts to middle-class workers, homeowners and retirees, saying if he was elected president he would "end the preferential treatment that's built into our tax code." Obama said he would give a $500 tax credit to more than 150 million workers, create a tax credit for homeowners who do not itemize their deductions and eliminate income taxes for older taxpayers who make less than $50,000 a year. To pay for the plan, he said he would raise capital gains taxes on the wealthy, close corporate loopholes and abolish tax breaks that have saved hedge fund and private equity managers billions of dollars.

"If you talk about this in polite company, sooner or later you'll get accused of waging class warfare," Obama said. "As if it's distasteful to point out that some C.E.O.'s make more in ten minutes than a worker makes in ten months."

Obama is an advocate for working Americans and argues against special interests that he says have contributed to a widening gap between the rich and the middle class and poor. He said the nation's "social compact is starting to crumble."

In an address to the nonpartisan Tax Policy Center, Obama also proposed major simplifications to the tax system, with a goal of making basic tax filing a five-minute exercise. For about forty million Americans without complex taxes, he said, the government would essentially send a bill based on electronic information from employers and banks. While Obama said he had not settled on how high to raise the capital gains rates, he added that he would "adjust the top dividends and capital gains rate to something closer to — but no greater than — the rates Ronald Reagan set in 1986."

Obama's plan would essentially increase tax rates on the wealthy and some corporations to reduce taxes on lower- and middle-income people. He called for a credit of $500 per person — or $1,000 per family — to offset some payroll taxes. Advisers said the credit would be phased out for income levels exceeding $150,000. The plan also called for extending a mortgage credit to taxpayers who do not itemize, generating about $500 in savings for ten million people. Finally, by eliminating income taxes for older Americans earning less than $50,000 a year, Obama said twenty-two million people would no longer need to file an income tax return. And seven million Americans, he said, would receive a tax cut of about $1,400.

Obama laid out his four-point strategy for Iraq on September 12, 2007, to a crowd at Ashton University in Clinton, Iowa. It comprised of: 1) Commencing in an immediate withdrawal of one or two brigades (3,500 or 7,000 troops) a month; 2) a pressing effort for political stability, with aid from a United Nations constitutional convention; 3) increased regional diplomacy, especially with leaders of Syria and Iran; and 4) humanitarian intervention and financial aid to help stem the effects of current and future sectarian violence.

Although the Obama plan called for a remaining residual military presence to protect American diplomatic and military personnel and continue hunting al-Qaeda, the Illinois senator did not, in his speech or in an extended overview of his plan, reveal exactly how many troops would remain. Obama was introduced by an Iraq veteran, who served in Fallujah, and spoke against a backdrop of American flags with a small sign on the podium that read, "Turning the Page in Iraq."

Obama's speech also included a few lightly veiled political digs at Hillary Clinton, invoking the term "conventional thinking" several times. In an unmistakable shot at Clinton, he said: "Despite -- or perhaps because of how much experience they had in Washington -- too many politicians feared looking weak and failed to ask hard questions. Too many took the President at his word instead of reading the intelligence for themselves." He also joked about the namesake of the city in which he was speaking, saying, "It was a happy accident, but we do hope that the headline after we leave is 'Clinton endorses Obama.'"

On December 8, 2007, Oprah Winfrey took the stage at William Bryce Football Stadium to deafening cheers. Over 29,000 people filled the risers, some having driven from as far as Savannah, GA, to see her appear with Barack Obama. At what was the third campaign stop Oprah made with Obama, she praised him as an "evolved leader," pinning her desire to support Obama on his ability to inspire people.

"For the first time, I'm stepping out of my pew because I've been inspired. I've been inspired to believe that a new vision is possible for America. Dr. King dreamed the dream. But we don't have to just dream the dream anymore. We get to vote that dream into reality," she told the crowd.

Her words appeared compelling against the background of a football stadium filled with people. Oprah's message was one of personal empowerment, similar to the stories she tells on her show every day, telling the crowd that asking Obama to wait to run was the same as someone telling someone that they should wait to try and better their lives. It played well with the crowd who shouted and applauded as she spoke and even joked, “I got some sense; I know the difference between a book club and this seminal moment in our history."

Obama also had a fine moment, bringing thousands to their feet saying that it was time to "stand up" for change. The event ended with the crowd dancing along with Obama, his wife Michelle and Oprah. But the pivotal moment for those watching came earlier, when Oprah ended her ringing endorsement by chanting "Barack Obama!" and dancing with Mrs. Obama on stage. Music from the band U2 swelled across the stadium, and Obama sauntered up to the stage, throwing his arms around both women and the three waved to the screaming crowd.

Jeremy Bird and Anton Gunn, the campaign's field and political directors, took the stage to ask the crowd to text their phone numbers to Obama's campaign. They also broke a Guinness World Record by conducting the world's largest phone bank, 36,426 people in the audience called four names of South Carolinian voters listed on the back of their tickets and asked them to support Barack Obama. According to the Obama campaign, eighteen percent of the first 8,500 people who signed into the event said they wanted to volunteer. Sixty-eight percent of people who got tickets online to the event had never been contacted by the campaign before.

The Obamas and Winfrey shook hands with supporters and left South Carolina for Manchester, NH to speak at the sold-out, 11,000-seat stadium there.

Photo courtesy Matthew Lawrence, Obama Staff Intern, Greenwood, South Carolina

William Bryce Football Stadium

Photo courtesy Matthew Lawrence, Obama Staff Intern, Greenwood, South Carolina

The line outside the stadium was already wrapped around the stadium at this point, not one but two times.

Photo courtesy Matthew Lawrence, Obama Staff Intern, Greenwood, South Carolina

Oprah greets fans after the appearance at William Bryce Football Stadium

Photo courtesy Matthew Lawrence, Obama Staff Intern, Greenwood, South Carolina
Obama interacts with supporters after an appearance at William Bryce Football Stadium.

On January 3, 2008, Obama won the Iowa caucus. A record turnout of voters embraced his promise of change, dealing a setback to Hillary Clinton in the nation's first caucuses. In fact, John Edwards came in second and Clinton came in third. Obama told the audience, "You have done what the cynics said you couldn't do. You have done what the state of New Hampshire can do in five days." Five days later, Obama lost the New Hampshire Democratic Primary. Later in the month, on January 26, Obama won South Carolina by thirty points, drawing a wide majority of black support and one-quarter of white voters. He bounced back from his losses in New Hampshire and Nevada to set the stage for the multistate fight of "Super Tuesday." Former President Bill Clinton compared Obama's victory to that of Jesse Jackson in 1984 and 1988. These comments damaged he and his wife's relationship with the black community at that time. The Obama campaign reported raising $32 million in the month of January alone through small donations by many donors.

More than 15,000 people swarmed Taco Bell Arena to hear Barack Obama speak to Idahoans on February 2, 2008. The doors opened at 7 a.m., and organizers had planned for about 8,800 people. They were reconfiguring the arena and opening up additional space to let even more people in.

"I've been around a long time, and I've seen a lot of political candidates come and go," former Governor Cecil D. Andrus said in introducing Obama. "I have not seen since John F. Kennedy in 1960, a candidate that has the capacity to unite and inspire the people of America like Barack Obama."

Saul Loeb/Agence France-Presse - Getty Images

Mr. Obama celebrating at a victory rally in Des Moines, Iowa

Jim Wilson/The New York Times

Michelle celebrates her husband’s victory at the convention center in Columbia, S.C.

Supporters listen to Obama's speech in Boise, Idaho.

Obama took the stage just after 9:10 a.m. "Thank you Boise! Thank you Idaho! What an unbelievable crowd," Obama said to wild cheers from the audience. The candidate thanked his supporters in Idaho - and even the folks that were not able to get inside. Speakers were set up outside so those who could not make it in could hear the speech. About 1,000 people were not able to get inside.

He hit many of the recurring themes of his campaign - including the faltering economy, the environment and the war in Iraq. The crowd behind Obama was filled with a wide variety of Idahoans - male and female, young and old.

"Change in America does not happen from the top down, it happens from the bottom up. I was certain that we are not as divided as our politics suggest," Obama said. "I believe that the American people are a decent people, and a hard-working people."

He repeatedly came back to the war in Iraq - and his plan to get American troops out of the country.

"All across the country, I meet veterans of Iraq and Afghanistan who are proud of their service, and properly so. But those veterans are thinking about those they left behind, and they question a mission that costs us more blood and treasure," Obama said.

He even referenced a recent story showing that he is a distant relative of current vice president Dick Cheney. "The name of my cousin Dick Cheney will not be on the ballot. That was really embarrassing when the news came out! When they do these surveys, you hope you're related to someone cool - Dick Cheney... that was really a letdown," Obama said to laughs.

The candidate says he will work to overhaul the health care system in America. "If you've got health care on the job, we'll work with your employer to lower your premiums by $2,500 every year. We will emphasize prevention so that we don't have children going to the emergency rooms for preventable illnesses like asthma."

Obama promised to have his health care plan in place by the end of his first term in office. He also said he will institute a plan to raise the minimum wage to keep pace - not "just every ten years. We can help rural communities build new schools. I won't just talk about how great teachers are, I will reward them by paying them higher salaries."

Obama said he would change the current system of accountability to eliminate "high stakes tests." He wants the educational system to focus on the humanities as well as core subjects. Obama touted his plan to give a $4,000 per student tuition credit to students, in exchange for community service and volunteerism time.

He would also work to put in place tougher emission standards, in an effort to cut down on petroleum use. He came back to the subject of Iraq several times throughout the speech, deriding the loss of lives, and the amount spent on the war. He called Iraq a distraction from the war in Afghanistan.

"We never finished that fight – and I intend to finish it when I am President of the United States," he said. "I opposed the war in Iraq from the start. This is why I'll put an end to the war and bring our troops home in 2009. I don't just want to end the war; I want to end the mindset that brought us to war. There was a time when people said 'well, maybe he's too nice.' Well, I said to them 'if you know who you are, and what you believe in - you can afford to reach out across the aisle.'"

Forty-four minutes after he started, Obama wrapped up at 9:54 a.m. with this: "This is our moment. This is our time. If you are willing to stand with me, if you are willing to caucus for me - if you believe this is not the end of the American Dream, but the beginning - if you believe we have to keep the dream alive, if you are not willing to settle - then I promise you we will not just win Idaho, we will not just win the nomination, we will win the general election and change this world!"

"Super Tuesday" is perhaps the most important Election Day in the U.S. primaries. It can make or break an election season for some candidates. Many believed that the early election period would end with this day on February 5, 2008. However, the results were inconclusive – Obama won more states while Clinton won more popular votes.

Prior to "Super Tuesday," Obama had sixty-three delegates while Clinton had forty-eight. To secure a nomination, a Democratic candidate must win at least 2,025 delegates. Twenty-four states held primaries or caucuses on this "Super Tuesday," with fifty-two percent of all pledge Democratic Party delegates at stake. Obama won thirteen states and 847 delegates and Clinton won nine states and 834 delegates on this date. This left Obama with 1,347 total delegates and Clinton with 1,219, neither enough to clinch the nomination.

On February 18, 2008, Michelle Obama commented in Milwaukee, Wisconsin that, "For the first time in my adult life, I am proud of my country because it feels like hope is finally making a comeback." Later that evening she reworded her stump speech in Madison, Wisconsin, saying "For the first time in my adult lifetime, I'm really proud of my country, and not just because Barack has done well, but because I think people are hungry for change." Several commentators criticized her for her remarks, and the campaign issued a statement that "anyone who heard her remarks ... would understand that she was commenting on our politics." In June 2008, Laura Bush indicated she thought Michelle Obama's words had been misrepresented in the media. "I think she probably meant I'm 'more proud,' you know, is what she really meant," adding, "I mean, I know that, and that's one of the things you learn and that's one of the really difficult parts both of running for president and for being the spouse of the president, and that is, everything you say is looked at and in many cases misconstrued."

Throughout the campaign, the media often labeled Michelle as an "angry black woman," causing her to respond: "Barack and I have been in the public eye for many years now, and we've developed a thick skin along the way. When you're out campaigning, there will always be criticism. I just take it in stride, and at the end of the day, I know that it comes with the territory."

Clinton's campaign on February 19, 2008, accused Obama of committing plagiarism in a portion of his speech delivered in Milwaukee, Wisconsin, from speeches written by Massachusetts Governor Deval Patrick. Obama told reporters he should have credited Patrick, a friend, for a passage in the speech, but that his rival was "carrying it too far."

"Let's see," Obama said. "I've written two books. I wrote most of my speeches. I would add that I noticed Senator Clinton, on occasion, has used words of mine as well."

The exchange injected a fresh dose of contention into the bitter fight for the Democratic nomination. Obama said two of his standard lines — "It's time to turn the page" and "Fired up and ready to go" — had made their way into Clinton's remarks, as well. One of Clinton's top advisers, Howard Wolfson, convened a conference call with reporters to accuse Obama of plagiarizing Patrick's remarks from a 2006 campaign appearance. Wolfson said it was important for voters to know that Obama's rhetoric, at least in this instance, was not original.

During a news conference here, Obama said he and Patrick "trade ideas all the time." Asked if he should have given credit to Patrick, he said, "I'm sure I should have," but he said he doubted that voters were concerned by the dust-up. "I'm happy to give Deval credit, as I give to a lot of people for spurring all kinds of ideas," he said. "But I think it's fair to say that everything we've been doing and generating excitement and the interest that people have had in the elections is based on the core belief in me that we need change in America."

The controversy arose after Obama delivered a speech at a Democratic Party dinner. He responded to criticism from Clinton, of New York, who argued that Obama might deliver smooth speeches, but that she was better prepared to solve problems.

"Don't tell me words don't matter," he said in his remarks. "'I have a dream.' Just words? 'We hold these truths to be self-evident that all men are created equal.' Just words? 'We have nothing to fear but fear itself.' Just words? Just speeches?"

The passage was similar to one used by Patrick in response to similar criticism. Patrick said he and Obama had discussed the argument in advance and he encouraged his friend to defend himself the same way he did during his race in 2006.

Antoin "Tony" Rezko, a former fundraiser for Obama, went on trial for corruption on March 3, 2008. He was accused of trying to extort millions of dollars in payoffs and campaign cash from companies aiming to do business with the state of Illinois. He was convicted on June 4, 2008, of federal charges of fraud and money laundering. The same day, the Republican National Committee sent a news release titled "Rezko: Obama's longtime friend and money man."

They implied that Rezko had helped Obama save $300,000 less than the asking price for the mansion he and Michelle purchased for $1.65 million in 2005. While the Obamas did pay $300,000 less than the asking price for the mansion, the seller, Frederic Wondisford, sent an e-mail posted by the Obama campaign stating the Obamas' offer of $1.65 million was the best offer he had received on the house and that the Obamas had given two lower offers that were rejected before they settled for that amount. The Republican Committee also claimed that "Obama has maintained a friendship with a now-convicted felon." Rezko had been a longtime friend of Obama's dating back to law school at Harvard. Obama was offered work in Rezko's development company – he declined. Their work overlapped occasionally but the two became friends when Obama first ran for Illinois State Senate as Rezko became a key supporter and fundraiser for Obama. However, in October, 2006, Rezko was indicted on the charges and Obama took all campaign contributions tied to Rezko - $160,000 in January, 2008 – and donated them to charity. Obama said that while Rezko is still considered a friend, he has not spoken to him since his indictment in 2006.

Barack Obama, the Democratic nominee for President, first met Reverend Jeremiah Wright and joined his church in the 1980s, while he was working as a community organizer in Chicago before attending Harvard Law School. Wright officiated at the wedding ceremony of Barack and Michelle Obama, as well as their children's baptism. The title of Obama's memoir, *The Audacity of Hope*, was inspired by one of Wright's sermons. Wright was scheduled to give the public invocation before Obama's presidential announcement, but Obama withdrew the invitation the night before the event. Wright wrote a rebuttal letter to the editor disputing the characterization of the account as reported in an article in *The New York Times*. In 2007, Wright was appointed to Barack Obama's African American Religious Leadership Committee, a group of over 170 national black religious leaders who supported Obama's bid for the Democratic nomination; however, it was announced in March 2008 that Wright was no longer serving as a member of this group.

During the period in which that announcement was made, a controversy broke out concerning Obama's long-term relationship with Wright, his former pastor. ABC News found several racially and politically charged sermons by Wright. Some of Wright's statements, such as when he said, "God Damn America," were widely interpreted as being unpatriotic and deeply offensive. Some have noted that Wright's quotes had been taken out of context, including in one case, where Wright was allegedly quoting Ambassador Edward Peck. Some have also noted that Dr. Martin Luther King, Jr. made similar comments about U.S. foreign policy and claimed that America was the "greatest purveyor of violence in the world today," and at another point King stated: "America was founded on genocide, and a nation that is founded on genocide is destructive."

Following negative media coverage and during a temporary drop in the polls, Obama responded by condemning Wright's remarks and delivering a speech entitled "A More Perfect Union" at the Constitution Center in Philadelphia, Pennsylvania. In the speech, Obama rejected Wright's comments, but refused to disown the man himself. Although the speech, which attempted to explain and contextualize the comments, was generally well-received, some continued to press the question of Obama's long-standing relationship with Wright. When asked his opinion of the controversy, Wright said, "I felt it was unfair. I felt it was unjust. I felt it was untrue. I felt for those who were doing that, were doing it for some very devious reasons. I think they wanted to... put an element of fear and hatred and to stir up the anxiety of Americans who still don't know the African-American tradition, know nothing about the prophetic theology of the African-American experience, who know nothing about the black church, who don't even know how we got a black church."

On April 27, Wright gave a keynote address at the 53rd Annual Fight for Freedom Fund Dinner for the Detroit chapter of the NAACP. In front of nearly 10,000, Wright gave a speech in which he referred to the controversy, saying, "I am not running for the Oval Office. I been running for Jesus a long, long time, and I'm not tired yet!" Wright argued that Americans were beginning to change their attitudes and perceptions about differences among societal groups. Citing linguistic, pedagogical, hermeneutic, and other differences, and contrasting varied musicologies, he sought to show how black culture is "different" but not "deficient," while saying that European-American culture has historically held it to be deficient, and punctuating his speech at numerous times with the dinner's annual theme "A Change Is Going to Come." Earlier that day, he delivered a sermon to 4,000 congregants at the Friendship-West Baptist Church in Dallas. On April 28, 2008, Wright made additional remarks, and also answered questions from reporters, at the National Press Club in Washington, D.C. He argued that his attention in the media was not only an attack on him, but also an attack on the black church in general. At a news conference the following day, Barack Obama decried Wright's latest remarks as "a bunch of rants that aren't grounded in the truth". He accused his former pastor of exploiting racism and "giving comfort to those who prey on hate." He characterized Wright's National Press Club appearance as a "spectacle" and described its content as "outrageous" and "destructive."

"After seeing Reverend Wright's performance, I felt there was a complete disregard for what the American people are going through and the need for them to rally together to solve these problems," he said. "What mattered to him was him commanding center stage." Obama said he was "particularly angered" by Wright's allegation that the candidate was engaging in political posturing when he denounced the minister's earlier remarks. "If Reverend Wright considers that political posturing, then he doesn't know me very well," Obama said. "Based on his comments yesterday, well, I may not know him as well as I thought, either."

On May 31, 2008, Obama announced that he had resigned from his membership in the Trinity United Church of Christ, of which Wright had previously served as pastor.

Ozier Muhammad/The New York Times

Mr. Obama announcing his decision to leave his church in Aberdeen, S.D.

New Mexico Governor Bill Richardson endorsed Obama on March 21, 2008, even though he had served in Clinton's administration. Having abandoned his own campaign for the presidency, he said Obama was an "extraordinary American" and that "Barack Obama will make a great and historic president. It's a once-in-a-lifetime opportunity for our nation and you are a once-in-a-lifetime leader." James Carville, a Clinton campaign advisor, called Richardson a "Judas" for his disloyalty while Clinton shrugged off his endorsement, saying it would be the voters who would decide, not the endorsers.

While Obama's rivals were calling for a national gas tax holiday, he dismissed it as a political ploy that wouldn't help struggling consumers. Clinton and Republican presidential nominee John McCain called for a holiday on collecting the federal gas tax "to get them through an election," Obama said. "The easiest thing in the world for a politician to do is tell you exactly what you want to hear." Clinton called for a windfall tax on oil companies to pay for a gas tax holiday but Obama disputed whether ending a collection of the gas tax is the quickest and best way to help consumers. The plan included suspending the collection of 18.4 cent federal gas tax 24.4 cent diesel tax for the summer of 2008. Obama said drying up gas tax collections would batter highway construction.

"We're arguing over a gimmick that would save you half a tank of gas over the course of the entire summer so that everyone in Washington can pat themselves on the back and say they did something," Obama said. He said his call for middle-class tax cuts would be far more beneficial than suspending gas tax collections.

Obama won North Carolina on May 6, 2008, by fourteen percentage points and over 200,000 votes. It was his first primary victory in nearly two months by that time. Clinton won Indiana narrowly, leading Obama's aides to claim the race's finish line was in view – "Following Obama's landslide victory in the North Carolina primary and his narrow defeat in Indiana, the media all but declare him the Democratic nominee – even though he hasn't won the necessary majority of delegates." At least three in five voters in both states said the economy was the most important problem facing the country, according to surveys of voters leaving polling places that were conducted in both states by Edison/Mitofsky for the television networks and The Associated Press. In Indiana, about eight in ten voters were white and about fifteen percent were black. Six in ten of the whites voted for Clinton; about nine in ten blacks favored Obama. Five days later, on May 11, Obama took the lead in the superdelegate count, which Clinton once led by nearly 100. Three days after that, John Edwards endorsed Obama.

More than 75,000 people gathered at an Obama rally in Waterfront Park in Portland, Oregon on May 18, 2008. Sixty-thousand people packed into a park on the banks of the Willamette River to hear Obama speak and another 15,000 people stood outside the gates while still hundreds more anchored in the river in their motorboats, kayaks, and canoes.

Portland is a Democratic stronghold, known for its bike paths and green ethos. It was one of the few cities in the country to briefly allow gay marriage, and frowns on plastic bags and chain restaurants alike. Demographically, Portland and its suburbs are stocked with the kinds of people who had been supporting Obama in droves: young, progressive, well-educated and financially stable. Portland is also overwhelmingly white, though Hispanic and Asian groups have a presence in the city. That deprived Obama of one of his most dependable voting groups, African-Americans.

Sen. Barack Obama, D-Ill., left, with his wife Michelle holding daughter Sasha, 6, as daughter Malia, 9, stands between, waves to a sea of supporters at a campaign rally on the banks of the Willamette River in Portland, Ore., Sunday, May 18, 2008.

Sen. Barack Obama, D-Ill., speaks to people at Waterfront Park in Portland, Ore.

Some voters lined up before dawn to see him, including Michelle Kay. "We are all so sick of Bush, his lies, the war," she said. "When Obama came out he was so honest, so refreshing."

Two days after the rally, on May 20, 2008, Obama declared he had enough superdelegates to win the Democratic nomination. He was confident of the support of approximately 120 of the remaining 260 undeclared superdelegates. He was right as on June 3, 2008, he clinched the Democratic nomination. The final primaries held in Montana and South Dakota and a last minute rush of superdelegates allowed him to claim victory, having won 2,118 delegates.

"Tonight, we mark the end of one historic journey with the beginning of another — a journey that will bring a new and better day to America," Obama told supporters at a rally in St. Paul. "Because of you, tonight I can stand here and say that I will be the Democratic nominee for president of the United States of America."

Obama's victory ended a sixteen-month primary campaign that broke records on several fronts: the number of voters who participated, the amount of money raised and spent and the sheer length of the fight. The campaign, infused by tensions over race and gender, provided unexpected twists to the end as Obama ultimately prevailed over Clinton, who just a year prior had appeared headed toward becoming the first female presidential nominee of a major party.

He was locked in a tight battle with Clinton until he became the presumptive nominee and Clinton ended her bid officially on June 4, 2008, urging her supporters to unite the Democratic Party by backing Obama for president.

On June 19, 2008, Obama became the first major-party presidential candidate to turn down public financing in the general election since the system was created in 1976. He reversed his pledge to seek public financing in the general election, passing up nearly $85 million in taxpayer money and instead looking to the 1.5 million donors who contributed to his primary campaign.

Ozier Muhammad/The New York Times

Senator Barack Obama with his wife, Michelle, in St. Paul.

Obama picked Senator Joe Biden to be his vice presidential running mate on August 22, 2008, and announced it through a late-night text message to supporters. His choice balanced his ticket with an older congressional veteran well-versed in foreign and defense issues.

Biden had twice sought the White House prior to being chosen. He is a Catholic with blue-collar roots and he has a generally liberal voting record. He had served at various times as chairman of the Foreign Relations Committee and as head of the Judiciary Committee and it was believed he could benefit Obama with the blue-collar vote he had lost to Clinton due to his working-class roots. He was sixty-five at the time Obama chose him as the vice presidential nominee and was elected into the Senate at the age of twenty-nine in 1973.

Obama formally introduced Biden as his vice presidential pick at a rally in Springfield, IL, on August 23, where he had previously announced his run for president. He said Biden was a man "ready to step in and be president." Both men spoke for 16 minutes and Obama's remarks were carefully crafted to emphasize Biden's accomplishments in the Senate, his blue-collar roots and -- above all -- his experience on foreign policy. "I can tell you Joe Biden gets it," he said. "He's that unique public servant who is at home in a bar in Cedar Rapids and the corridors of the Capitol, in the VFW hall in Concord, and at the center of an international crisis," he said.

Although Obama's campaign had promised supporters who turned over their phone numbers they would be the first to know who Obama had chosen via text message, his choice had been leaked to the media several hours prior. The campaign scrambled to send the text message after the leak, causing some supporters on the East Coast to get the message just after three in the morning.

The official logo released after the V.P. announcement.

Democratic Presidential Dream Team, 2008 – Barack Obama and his V.P. choice Senator Joe Biden at the announcement rally in Springfield, Ill.

Barack Obama with wife Michelle and Joe Biden with wife Jill.

On August 28, 2008, Senator Barack Obama accepted the Democratic Party's nomination in front of nearly 85,000 people at the Democratic National Convention in Denver, Colorado. In remarks provided by the Obama campaign, Obama accepted the nomination "with profound gratitude and great humility." He laid out his economic, foreign, and domestic policies before a roaring crowd at Invesco Field. The speech concluded the fourth and final night of the 2008 DNC and was given on the forty-fifth anniversary of Dr. Martin Luther King's "I Have a Dream" speech. In Obama's speech, he stated that the "American people has been threatened" by eight years under President George W. Bush and that John McCain represented a continuation of policies that undermined the nation's economy and imperiled its standing around the world. He addressed his plans and policies never heard before in past speeches to the thousands of people at the Convention and to over thirty-eight million Americans watching the speech, an American television record for viewership during a convention. This is an excerpt from that speech:

> Four years ago, I stood before you and told you my story - of the brief union between a young man from Kenya and a young woman from Kansas who weren't well-off or well-known, but shared a belief that in America, their son could achieve whatever he put his mind to.
>
> It is that promise that has always set this country apart - that through hard work and sacrifice, each of us can pursue our individual dreams but still come together as one American family, to ensure that the next generation can pursue their dreams as well.
>
> That's why I stand here tonight. Because for two hundred and thirty two years, at each moment when that promise was in jeopardy, ordinary men and women - students and soldiers, farmers and teachers, nurses and janitors — found the courage to keep it alive.
>
> We meet at one of those defining moments - a moment when our nation is at war, our economy is in turmoil, and the American promise has been threatened once more.
>
> Tonight, more Americans are out of work and more are working harder for less. More of you have lost your homes and even more are watching your home values plummet. More of you have cars you can't afford to drive, credit card bills you can't afford to pay, and tuition that's beyond your reach.
>
> These challenges are not all of government's making. But the failure to respond is a direct result of a broken politics in Washington and the failed policies of George W. Bush.

America, we are better than these last eight years. We are a better country than this.

This country is more decent than one where a woman in Ohio, on the brink of retirement, finds herself one illness away from disaster after a lifetime of hard work.

This country is more generous than one where a man in Indiana has to pack up the equipment he's worked on for twenty years and watch it shipped off to China, and then chokes up as he explains how he felt like a failure when he went home to tell his family the news.

We are more compassionate than a government that lets veterans sleep on our streets and families slide into poverty; that sits on its hands while a major American city drowns before our eyes.

Tonight, I say to the American people, to Democrats and Republicans and Independents across this great land - enough! This moment - this election - is our chance to keep, in the 21st century, the American promise alive. Because next week, in Minnesota, the same party that brought you two terms of George Bush and Dick Cheney will ask this country for a third. And we are here because we love this country too much to let the next four years look like the last eight. **On November 4th, we must stand up and say: "Eight is enough."**

CHAPTER 11 – PRESIDENT-ELECT BARACK OBAMA

On the morning of Election Day, Tuesday, November 4, 2008, Barack Obama cast his vote in Chicago, Illinois within their first hour of opening. Senator Biden cast his vote at 2:30 in the afternoon. That evening, all American networks called the election in favor of Barack Obama at 11:00 P.M. Eastern Standard Time as the polls closed on the west coast with the electoral vote totals between 297 for Obama and 146 for McCain. It was in no way a landslide victory for Senator Obama, with only 270 electoral votes needed to win the nomination and Senator McCain trailing significantly behind throughout the evening. Senator McCain gave a concession speech half an hour later while President-elect Barack Obama appeared at midnight Eastern time, November 5, in Grant Park in front of a crowd of two-hundred fifty thousand people to deliver his acceptance speech. Following his speech, spontaneous street parties broke out in major cities across the world such as New York, Toronto, Miami, Rio de Janeiro, Chicago, Sydney, Detroit, Berlin, Boston, Kenya, Seattle, London, Philadelphia, and Washington D.C. Television coverage of the 2008 U.S. Election results drew more than seventy-one million average viewers, according to Nielsen. In the end, Obama received 365 electoral votes, or 53% of the vote with 66,882, 230 votes and McCain received 173 electoral votes or 46% of the vote with 58,343,671 votes.

America's new first-family greets the crowd of 250,000 people in Grant Park, November 4, 2008.

Vice President Joe Biden and wife, Jill, join the Obamas on Election Night in Grant Park, November 4, 2008.

Prior to the election, commentators discussed whether Senator Obama would be able to redraw the electoral map by winning states that had been voting for Republican candidates in recent decades. In many ways, he was successful. He won every region of the country by double digits except the South, which the Republicans won by less than double digits (nine points). He won Delaware, Maryland, North Carolina, Florida, and Virginia in the South. The Republicans "took the South only because McCain, who ran roughly even with Obama among whites in every other region, won Southern whites by thirty-eight percentage points." Obama was the first Democratic Presidential nominee to carry Virginia and Indiana since 1964, and the first to carry North Carolina since 1976. Obama was also able to win one electoral vote from Nebraska (together with Maine, one of two states that split their electoral votes), winning the electoral vote from Nebraska's 2nd congressional district. Nebraska's other four electoral votes went to John McCain.

At the same time, Senator Obama defied several bellwethers; Obama was the first Democratic nominee since Woodrow Wilson in 1916 to win the presidency without winning West Virginia. He was also the first to win the presidency without winning five or more states of the South. Barack Obama was the first president since 1968 to win the presidency without winning Arkansas and Louisiana, as well as Kentucky and Tennessee since 1960. Missouri also went for McCain, making 2008 the first time since 1956 that the state did not vote for the winner of the presidential race.

A number of pre-election controversies revolved around challenges to voter registration lists, involving techniques such as caging lists alleged to constitute voter suppression. There were even reports of phone calls made to Obama supporters in which it was said the polls were too overwhelmed and that Democrats must vote on November 5 while only Republicans could vote November 4. Reporter Greg Palast predicted many 2004 United States election voting controversies could recur. Voter list purges using unlawful criteria caused controversy in at least six swing states: Colorado, Indiana, Ohio, Michigan, Nevada and North Carolina. On October 5, 2008 the Republican Lt. Governor of Montana, John Bohlinger, accused the Montana Republican Party of vote caging to purge 6,000 voters from three counties which trend Democratic. Allegations arose in Michigan that the Republican Party planned to challenge the eligibility of voters based on lists of foreclosed homes. The Obama campaign filed a lawsuit challenging this. The House Judiciary Committee wrote to the Department of Justice requesting an investigation.

Photo courtesy of Ivin Nitkin.

A crowd of over 250,000 people gathered to see Obama's acceptance speech in Grant Park in Chicago, IL on Election Night, November 4, 2008.

The McCain campaign tried to publicize the alleged ACORN scandal, in which the voter registration organization reported a small percentage of strange names among those they registered (many of whom were reportedly Democrats). Several states investigated allegations of fraud but did not find the organization liable. Voter fraud would not take place unless someone tried to vote using one of the illegal names.

Virginia election authorities were ordered by a federal judge to preserve late-arriving absentee ballots sent by active-duty military personnel following a suit by the McCain campaign. It alleged that the state sent absentee ballots late to servicemen. According to federal law, absentee ballots must be mailed to troops in foreign countries at least forty-five days prior to an election. The charge against Virginia was that the ballots were not printed until after the deadline and therefore were mailed late to soldiers abroad.

Guam's 173,000 residents are U.S. citizens, and must obey U.S. laws passed in Washington, yet they have neither a voting member of Congress, nor votes in the Electoral College. Since 1980 they have held a straw poll for president at the same time as the U.S. national elections. In 2007, Guam's legislature voted to move the straw poll up to September, to draw attention to the choices of Guam's population, as well as their continued disfranchisement, but the bill was vetoed by the governor. Obama won the 2008 Guam Straw Poll by 20,120 votes to 11,940 for McCain.

Obama's acceptance speech in Grant Park in Chicago drew a crowd of 250,000 people. Tickets were made available on his social networking website and within hours of members receiving the e-mail to sign up for tickets, they were gone. Street vendors sold buttons, t-shirts, American flags, photos, and other Obama memorabilia to those headed to Grant Park. His speech focused on major issues facing the United States and the world and referenced the inaugural addresses of Presidents John F. Kennedy and Abraham Lincoln. He also referred to the speeches of Martin Luther King, Jr. He declared, "But tonight, because of what we did on this day, in this election, at this moment, change has come to America," and "The road ahead will be long, our climb will be steep. We may not get there in one year, or even in one term – but America, I have never been more hopeful than I am tonight that we will get there," echoing King's "I've Been to the Mountaintop" address. At another point in the speech, he again referenced King when referring to the "arc of history," a phrase King used regularly. He directly quoted Lincoln's first inaugural address in saying, "As Lincoln said to a nation far more divided than ours, we are not enemies but friends. Though passion may have strained, it must not break our bonds of affection." He also said, "It's been a long time coming, but…change has come to America," which is an allusion to the song by artist Sam Cooke called "A Change is Gonna Come." He made a humorous statement to his daughters about the next First Dog, saying, "Sasha and Malia…I love you both more than you can imagine. And you have earned the new puppy that's coming with us…to the White House." Since then, iReporters on CNN.com have been heavily speculating and recommending the breed of dog that will be chosen.

In addition to the tributes Obama paid to those who played a part in his history by quoting them, he spoke of the core issues facing the country today, including the economy, the war in Iraq, and the onset of global warming.

Photo courtesy of Ali Lueder.

A woman at Chicago's Grant Park shows her dislike for the past eight years and her support for Obama on November 4, 2008.

Rev. Jesse Jackson listens to President-elect Obama's acceptance speech.

Oprah Winfrey, a supporter of Obama's, waits for his acceptance speech while chatting and laughing with newly made friends.

Obama greets the crowd behind two pieces of bulletproof glass.

President-elect Barack Obama is seen on a large monitor at his election night rally in Grant Park.

He said, “Even as we stand here tonight, we know there are brave Americans waking up in the deserts of Iraq and the mountains of Afghanistan to risk their lives for us. There are mothers and fathers who will lie awake after the children fall asleep and wonder how they'll make the mortgage or pay their doctor's bills or save enough for their child's college education.” On the economic crisis in America, he said, “Let us remember that, if this financial crisis taught us anything, it's that we cannot have a thriving Wall Street while Main Street suffers.” And in a message to America's enemies, he said, “To those — to those who would tear the world down: We will defeat you. To those who seek peace and security: We support you. And to all those who have wondered if America's beacon still burns as bright: Tonight we proved once more that the true strength of our nation comes not from the might of our arms or the scale of our wealth, but from the enduring power of our ideals: democracy, liberty, opportunity and unyielding hope.” Obama's speech also marked the first time a President-elect referred to gay Americans in an acceptance speech.

Obama also reflected on the hard times of the campaign and the “challenges that America would face ahead.” Television coverage of the speech showed Jesse Jackson and Oprah Winfrey weeping in the crowd. One of the primary references within Obama's speech was to Ann Nixon Cooper, a 106-year-old resident of Atlanta, Georgia. He said, “She was born just a generation past slavery; a time when there were no cars on the road or planes in the sky, when someone like her couldn't vote for two reasons — because she was a woman and because of the color of her skin.” Obama also made reference to his popular campaign chant, *Yes We Can*: “And tonight, I think about all that she's seen throughout her century in America — the heartache and the hope; the struggle and the progress; the times we were told that we can't; and the people who pressed on with that American creed: 'Yes, we can.'”

Photo courtesy of Ogden Curtis.

Obama supporters celebrate the announcement of his election in Grant Park in Chicago, November 4, 2008.

Due to the high security threat involved, Obama delivered the speech protected by two pieces of bulletproof glass (two inches thick, ten feet high, fifteen feet long) to each side of the lectern to deflect any shots from the skyscrapers overlooking Grant Park. There was no glass shield in front of the lectern. A no-fly zone was also imposed over the area, with only police helicopters allowed in the air. The gathering involved the deployment of thousands of police, Army and Secret Service personnel. The event cost the Obama campaign an estimated $2 million.

The venue for Obama's speech was significant as Grant Park is the location of the 1968 Democratic National Convention, an event significant for its protests which ended in violence, riots and police brutality. CNN declared, "History gave Grant Park another chance Tuesday as the scene of a peaceful and jubilant celebration of Barack Obama's presidential victory." Obama's speech has been praised as having "...the rare ability to cultivate the things that are common to all human beings, regardless of artificial and arbitrary distinctions."

The crowd leaves Grant Park after Obama's acceptance speech, November 4, 2008.

Barack Obama has met with President George Bush and taken Malia and Sasha on a tour of their new home. He has also put his Presidential cabinet into place and is making the transition from Senator and Presidential candidate to President-elect of the United States of America. Obama will be inaugurated on January 20, 2009. The United States Constitution mandates that Obama make the following oath before he can "enter on the Execution" of the office of the presidency:

I do solemnly swear that I will faithfully execute the Office of President of the United States, and will to the best of my Ability, preserve, protect and defend the Constitution of the United States.

-INDEX-

-BIBLIOGRAPHY-

PREFACE
SOURCES

NEWSPAPERS:

Scharnberg, Kirsten and Kim Barker. "The Not-So-Simple Story of Barack Obama's Youth," *Chicago Tribue*, 25 March 2007.

CHAPTER I
SOURCES

BOOKS:

Auset Bakhufu. *Six Black Presidents: Black Blood, White Masks,* Temple Hills: Pik2 Publications, 1993.

ONLINE RESOURCES:

Black Woman Details Ties to Warren G. Harding. 5 February 2008. Pittsburg Post-Gazette. 29 August 2008. <http://www.post-gazette.com>.

John Hanson. Virtual War Museum. 7 July 2008. <http://www.johnhanson.net>.

Racial Heritage of Six Former Presidents Is Questioned. 5 February 2008. Pittsburg Post-Gazette. 29 August 2008. <http://www.post-gazette.com>.

The Genes That Build America. 15 July 2007. The Observer. 20 August 2008. <http://www.guardian.co.uk>.

CHAPTER II
SOURCES

BOOKS:

Obama, Barack. *Dreams from My Father: A Story of Race and Inheritance,* New York: Crown, 2007.

Obama, Barack. *The Audacity of Hope: Thoughts on Reclaiming the American Dream,* New York: Crown, 2006.

NEWSPAPERS:

Helman, Scott. "Small College Awakened Future Senator to Service," *The Boston Globe,* 25 August 2008.

ONLINE RESOURCES:

Barack Obama. 9 September 2008. Wikipedia. 14 September 2008. <http://www.wikipedia.org>.

Behind the Scenes: Meet George Obama. 23 August 2008. CNN. 25 August 2008. <http://www.cnn.com>.

Old Friends Recall Obama's Years in L.A., N.Y. 15 May 2008. Huffington Post. 10 August 2008. <http://www.huffingtonpost.com>.

CHAPTER III
SOURCES

BOOKS:

Obama, Barack. *Dreams from My Father: A Story of Race and Inheritance,* New York: Crown, 2007.
Obama, Barack. *The Audacity of Hope: Thoughts on Reclaiming the American Dream,* New York: Crown, 2006.

NEWSPAPERS:

Brown, Sarah. "Obama '85 Masters Balancing Act," *Daily Princetonian,* 7 December 2005.
Herrmann, Andrew. "Fame Puts Squeeze on Family Life," *Chicago Sun-Times*, 19 October 2006.
Slevin, Peter. "Her Heart's in the Race," *Washington Post*, 28 November 2007.
Sweet, Lynn. "Michelle Obama Quits Board of Wal-Mart Supplier," *Chicago Sun-Times,* 22 May 2007.
West, Cassandra. "Her Plan Went Awry, but Michelle Obama Doesn't Mind," *Chicago Tribune*, 1 September 2004.

ONLINE RESOURCES:

Meet Michelle. Obama for America. 7 November 2007. <http://www.barackobama.com>.
Michelle Obama. 27 August 2008. Wikipedia. 28 August 2008. <http://www.wikipedia.org>.
Michelle Obama Appointed Vice President. 9 May 2005. The University of Chicago Medical Center. 20 January 2008. <http://www.uchospitals.edu>.
The Woman Behind Obama. 20 January 2007. Chicago Sun-Times. 15 November 2007. <http://www.suntimes.com>.
Who is Michelle Obama? 25 January 2007. DiversityInc. 11 November 2007. <http://www.diversityinc.com>.

CHAPTER IV
SOURCES

ONLINE RESOURCES:

ABC News: Shirley Chisholm. 31 January 2006. ABC News. 17 August 2008. <http://abcnews.go.com>.
Shirley Chisholm. 2008. Answers.com. 17 August 2008. <http://www.answers.com>.
Shirley Chisholm. 4 March 2008. Citizendium. 17 August 20008. <http://en.citizendium.org>.
Shirley Chisholm. 12 September 2008. Wikipedia. 15 September 2008. <http://www.wikipedia.org>.

CHAPTER V
SOURCES

ONLINE RESOURCES:

Dick Gregory. 8 September 2008. Wikipedia. 15 September 2008. <http://www.wikipedia.org>.
Dick Gregory: Global Watch. 10 December 2007. <http://www.dickgregory.com>.

CHAPTER VI
SOURCES

ONLINE RESOURCES:

Black History – Jesse Jackson. 2001. Gale Group. 15 September 2008. <http://www.gale.cengage.com>.
Jesse Jackson. 6 September 2008. Wikipedia. 15 September 2008. <http://www.wikipedia.org>.

CHAPTER VII
SOURCES

ONLINE RESOURCES:

Amb. Carol Moseley Braun. 15 January 2004. Democracy in Action. 15 September 2008. <http://www.gwu.edu>.
Carol Moseley Braun. 2 September 2008. Wikipedia. 15 September 2008. <http://www.wikipedia.org>.

CHAPTER VIII
SOURCES

NEWSPAPERS:

Scott, Janny. "In 2000, a Streetwise Veteran Schooled a Bold Young Obama," *The New York Times*, 9 September 2007.

CHAPTER IX
SOURCES

BOOKS:

Bernstein, Carl. *A Woman in Charge: The Life of Hillary Rodham Clinton,* New York: Knopf, 2007.
Brock, David. *The Seduction of Hillary Rodham*, New York: Simon & Schuster, 2006.
Clinton, Hillary Rodham. *Living History,* New York: Simon & Schuster, 2003.
Gerth, Jeff; Don Van Natta, Jr. *Her Way: The Hopes and Ambitions of Hillary Rodham Clinton,* New York: Little, Brown and Company, 2007.

Graff, Henry Franklin. *The Presidents: A Reference History*, New York: Simon & Schuster, 2002.
Kearney, Janis F. *Conversations: William Jefferson Clinton, from Hope to Harlem*, Little Rock: Writing Our World Press, 2006.
Lindsay, Rae. *The Presidents' First Ladies*, Englewood Cliffs: R & R Writers/Agents, 2001.
Maraniss, David. *First In His Class: A Biography of Bill Clinton,* New York: Simon & Schuster, 1995.
Middendorf, J. William. *Glorious Disaster: Barry Goldwater's Presidential Campaign And the Origins of the Conservative Movement*, New York: Basic Books, 2006.
Morris, Roger. *Partners in Power: The Clintons and Their America*, New York: Henry Holt, 1996.
Olson, Barbara. *Hell to Pay: The Unfolding Story of Hillary Rodham Clinton*, Washington D.C.: Regnery Publishing, 1999.
Postrel, Virginia. *The Substance of Style: How the Rise of Aesthetic Value Is Remaking Commerce, Culture, and Consciousness*, New York: HarperCollins, 2004.
Troy, Gil. *Hillary Rodham Clinton: Polarizing First Lady*, Lawrence: University Press of Kansas, 2006.

NEWSPAPERS:

Archibold, Randal C. "Hillary Clinton Is Endorsed By Sierra Club as Better Ally," *The New York Times*, 6 September 2000.
Balz, Dan. "Hillary Clinton Crafts Centrist Stance on War," *The Washington Post*, 12 December 2005.
Barbaro, Michael. "As a Director, Clinton Moved Wal-Mart Board, but Only So Far," *The New York Times*, 20 May 2007.
Brooks, David. "The Center Holds," *The New York Times*, 25 September 2007.
Dowd, Maureen. "Can Hillary Upgrade?" *The New York Times*, 2 October 2002.
Dowd, Maureen. "Hillary Clinton as Aspiring First Lady: Role Model, or a 'Hall Monitor' Type?" *The New York Times*, 18 May 1992.
Fitzgerald, Jim. "Hillary Clinton says immediate withdrawal from Iraq would be 'a big mistake'," *Associated Press*, 21 November 2005.
Fouhy, Beth. "Hillary Claims Credit for Child Program," *Associated Press*, 7 October 2005.
Gerstein, Josh. "Hillary Clinton's Left Hook," *The New York Sun*, 27 November 2007.
Gerstein, Josh. "Hillary Clinton's Radical Summer," *The New York Sun*, 26 November 2007.
Gerstein, Josh. "The Clintons' Berkeley Summer of Love," *The New York Sun*, 26 November 2007.
Gerth, Jeff. "Clintons Joined S. & L. Operator in an Ozark Real-Estate Venture," *The New York Times*, 8 March 1992.
Gerth, Jeff, Don Van Natta, Jr.. "Hillary's War," *The New York Times Magazine*, 29 May 2007.
Gerth, Jeff, others. "Top Arkansas Lawyer Helped Hillary Clinton Turn Big Profit," *The New York Times*, 18 March 1994.
Greenhouse, Steven. "Hillary Clinton Stars, Unrivaled, at Labor Day Parade," *The New York Times*, 10 September 2000.
Groppe, Maureen. "Alito filibuster fails; Bayh, Lugar split," *The Indianapolis Star*, 31 January 2006.
Hakim, Danny. "Hillary, Not as in the Mount Everest Guy," *The New York Times*, 17 October 2006.
Healy, Patrick. "To Avoid Conflicts, Clintons Liquidate Holdings," *The New York Times*, 15 June 2007.
Hunt, Albert R. "A Tale of Two Clintons," *Wall Street Journal*, 7 April 2001.
Jackson, David. "First ladies often involved in husband's foreign policy," *USA Today*, 9 October 2007.
Jordan, Lara Jakes. "Clinton to return $850,000 raised by Hsu," *Associated Press*, 10 September 2007.
Kirkpatrick, David D. "As Clinton Runs, Some Old Foes Stay on Sideline," *The New York Times*, 19 February 2007.
Kornblut, Anne E., Dan Balz. "Clinton Regroups As Rivals Pounce," *The Washington Post*, 1 November 2007.
Kornblut, Anne E., Jeff Zeleny. "Clinton Won Easily, but Bankroll Shows the Toll," *The New York Times,* 21 November 2006.

Kuhnhenn, Jim. "Clinton to Give Away Fundraiser's Cash," *Associated Press*, 29 August 2007.
Lake, Eli. "Clinton Spars With Petraeus on Credibility," *The New York Sun*, 12 September 2007.
Leibovich, Mark. "In Turmoil of '68, Clinton Found a New Voice," *The New York Times*, 7 September 2007.
Levy, Clifford J. "Clinton Rivals Raise Little Besides Rage," *The New York Times*, 27 October 2000.
McIntire, Mike, Leslie Wayne. "Clinton Donor Under a Cloud In Fraud Case," *The New York Times*, 30 August 2007.
Morain, Dan. "Clinton leads the field in campaign fundraising," *The Los Angeles Times*, 2 October 2007.
Nagourney, Adam. "In a Kennedy's Legacy, Lessons and Pitfalls For Hillary Clinton; Carpetbagger Issue Has Echoes of '64, But Differences Could Prove Crucial," *The New York Times*, 10 September 2000.
Nagourney, Adam. "With Some Help, Clintons Purchase a White House," *The New York Times*, 3 September 1999.
Purdum, Todd S. "The First Lady's Newest Role: Newspaper Columnist," *The New York Times*, 24 July 1995.
Rosett, Claudia. "Hillary's Bull Market," *The Wall Street Journal*, 26 October 2000.
Turner, Douglas. "Clinton wants increase in size of regular Army," *The Buffalo News*, 14 July 2005.
Tyler, Patrick. "Hillary Clinton, In China, Details Abuse of Women," *The New York Times*, 6 September 1995
Woodward, Bob. "A Prosecutor Bound by Duty," *The Washington Post*, 15 June 1999.
Zeleny, Jeff. "Obama Raised $32.5 Million in Second Quarter," *The New York Times*, 1 July 2007.

ONLINE RESOURCES:

About Hillary. Friends of Hillary. 15 August 2008. <http://www.hillaryclinton.com>.
Biography of Hillary Clinton. The White House. 15 August 2008. <http://www.whitehouse.gov>.
Clinton Burnishes Hawkish Image. 14 July 2005. MSNBC. 23 August 2006. <http://www.msnbc.com>.
Clinton Shouldn't Worry Just About IA. 12 September 2007. MSNBC. 12 July 2007. <http://www.msnbc.com>.
Hillary Clinton Launches White House Bid: "I'm In." 22 January 2007. CNN. 05 February 2007. <http://www.cnn.com>.
Hillary Clinton: Midas Touch at Work. 04 September 2007. MSN. 19 September 2007. <http://www.msn.com>.
Hillary Clinton's Education. Hillary Clinton. 22 August 2006.
Hillary Launches Web Effort to Oust Gonzales. 14 March 2007. Newsmax. 24 March 2007. <http://www.newsmax.com>.
Hillary vs. Hillary. 26 October 2006. Snopes. 23 November 2007. <http://www.snopes.com>.
Paula Jones Challenges Clinton to Debate. 30 June 2004. CNN. 25 September 2007. <http://www.cnn.com>.
Poll: Liberals Moving Toward Clinton; GOP Race Tightens. 07 May 2007. CNN. 08 May 2007. <http://www.cnn.com>.
Reading Hillary Rodham's Hidden Thesis. 02 March 2007. MSNBC. 02 March 2007. <http://www.msnbc.com>.
Record Millions Roll in for Clinton White House Bid. 01 April 2007. CNN. 02 April 2007. <http://www.cnn.com>.
Senate Passes War Spending Bill With Withdrawal Deadline. 29 March 2007. CNN. 29 March 2007. <http://www.cnn.com>.
Senator Hillary Rodham Clinton: Biography. U.S. Senate. 15 August 2008. <http://clinton.senate.gov>.

CHAPTER X
SOURCES

BOOKS:

Obama, Barack. *Dreams from My Father: A Story of Race and Inheritance,* New York: Crown, 2007.
Obama, Barack. *The Audacity of Hope: Thoughts on Reclaiming the American Dream,* New York: Crown, 2006

NEWSPAPERS:

Ambinder, Marc. "Obama's Tax Plan: The Politics and Policy," *The Atlantic*, 18 September 2007.
Benn, Alvin and Jamie Kizzire. "Clinton, Obama Praise Civil Rights Achievements," *USA Today*, 4 March 2007.
Healy, Patrick and Jeff Zeleny. "Obama Outshines Clinton at Raising Funds," *The New York Times*, 8 February 2008.
Zeleny Jeff. "Clinton Camp Says Obama Plagiarized Speech," *The New York Times*, 19 February 2008.
Zeleny, Jeff. "Obama Clinches Nomination, First Black Candidate to Lead a Major Party Ticket," *The New York Times*, 4 June 2008.

ONLINE RESOURCES:

About 30,000 See Obama-Oprah in S.C. 09 December 2007. MSNBC. 13 December 2007. <http://www.msnbc.com.>
Jesse Jackson Endorses Obama For '08. 29 March 2007. Huffington Post. 04 April 2007. <http://www.huffingtonpost.com>.
Obama Placed Under Secret Service Protection. 3 May 2007. CNN. 8 May 2007. <http://www.cnn.com>.
Obama Raises $32.5 Million, Thought To Be a Democratic Party Record. 1 July 2007. CNN. 15 July 2007. <http://www.cnn.com>.
Obama Speaks to Big Crowd in Boise. 2 February 2008. KTVB. 5 February 2008. <http://www.ktvb.com>.
Obama's Iraq Plan. 12 September 2007. MSNBC. 20 September 2007. <http://www.msnbc.com>.
Rally for Barack Obama Draws Roughly 75,000 to Waterfront Park. 22 May 2008. Associated Press. 26 May 2008. <http://www.katu.com>.

- CREDITS-

Research Credits:
Dempsey Travis
Sherrol Glover
Heather Olson

Cover Design:
Dempsey Travis
Sherrol Glover

Cover Illustration; Editor; Typeset/Layout:
Heather Olson

-Other Books by Dempsey J. Travis-

Harold: The People's Mayor
This is a book for the many thousands of Chicagoans who revere the late MayorHarold Washington, who seems destined to become more legendary with each passing year. Travis may be the only writer in America who regularly sat down with Washington for long, tape recorded interviews. For those who want to reliveWashington's three mayoral campaigns, the book provides an extensive blow by blow account. — *Chicago Tribune*

Catalog Card# 0-941484-08-4
349pp/200 illus Cloth 6 3.8 x 9 ½

Racism: American Style
In this book, Chicago author Dempsey Travis captures the personal struggle of African American executives and other professionals to overcome racism and achieve their full potential. It is based in 122 interviews with Black men and women who have endured racism in Fortune 500 corporations, prestigious universities, leading hospitals, the military, the media, the banking industry, employment agencies, religion and country clubs. The anguish, rage, fear, shock and despair described by these veterans in the battle against racism grabs the reader on an emotional level and does not let go.
— *Chicago Tribune*

Catalog Card #0-941484-09-2
230pp Cloth 6 3/8 x 9 1/2"

An Autobiography of Black Chicago
Travis is an unbashed Black Horatio Alger and this is history as an object lesson, pure and simple. He earns your respect as well as your affection with his humorous observations on the Travis household, and in an age when a two-hour television movie is devoted to the exploits of a demented sociopath whose only accomplishment was the bungling of a third-rate burglary. Travis' writing is surprisingly free of anger at the thousand petty injustices that sear the soul of Black America.
— *Chicago Journal*

Catalog Card# 0-91484-01-7
400pp/150 illus Paper 6 3/8 x 9 1/2"

An Autobiography of
Black Politics

This book is a comprehensive political analysis of Blacks in the Illinois political structure. The work contains considerable empirical and analytic detail about the operation of Black politics at both the municipal and state level. A monumental work...the kind of book that I hope is read throughout the country.
— *Mayor Harold Washington*

Catalog Card # 0-941494-05-X
704pp/400 illus Cloth 7 1/2 x 9 ½

Order these great books and others at http://www.urbanresearchpress.com!!